# Moral Disagreement

In this book, Folke Tersman explores what we can learn about the nature of moral thinking from moral disagreement. He explains how diversity of opinion on moral issues undermines the idea that moral convictions can be objectively true or valid. Such arguments are often criticized for not being able to explain why there is a contrast between ethics and other areas in which there is disagreement, but where one does not give up the idea of an objective truth, as in the natural sciences. Tersman shows that the contrast has to do with facts about when, and on what basis, moral convictions can be correctly attributed to an agent or speaker.

Folke Tersman is a professor of philosophy at Stockholm University. In addition to articles in international journals such as *Erkenntnis, Synthese, Philosophical Quarterly, Philosophical Studies*, and *Theoria*, he is the author of several books on moral philosophy in Swedish.

T0372689

CAMBRIDGE STUDIES IN PHILOSOPHY

*General editor* ERNEST SOSA (Brown University)

*Advisory editors:*
JONATHAN DANCY (University of Reading)
JOHN HALDANE (University of St. Andrews)
GILBERT HARMAN (Princeton University)
FRANK JACKSON (Australian National University)
WILLIAM G. LYCAN (University of North Carolina at Chapel Hill)
SYDNEY SHOEMAKER (Cornell University)
JUDITH J. THOMSON (Massachusetts Institute of Technology)

# Moral Disagreement

FOLKE TERSMAN

*Stockholm University*

CAMBRIDGE
UNIVERSITY PRESS

CAMBRIDGE UNIVERSITY PRESS
Cambridge, New York, Melbourne, Madrid, Cape Town, Singapore, São Paulo, Delhi

Cambridge University Press
32 Avenue of the Americas, New York, NY 10013-2473, USA

www.cambridge.org
Information on this title: www.cambridge.org/9780521115551

First published 2006
This digitally printed version 2009

*A catalog record for this publication is available from the British Library*

*Library of Congress Cataloging in Publication data*
Tersman, Folke.
Moral disagreement / Folke Tersman.
p.   cm. – (Cambridge studies in philosophy)
Includes bibliographical references and index.
ISBN 0-521-85338-9
1. Ethics.   I. Title.   II. Series.
BJ1031.T47   2006
170′.42–dc22          2005012020

ISBN 978-0-521-85338-5 hardback
ISBN 978-0-521-11555-1 paperback

# Contents

# *Preface*

On June 22, 2000, Gary Graham was executed by lethal injection in the state prison of Huntsville, Texas, after nineteen years on death row. The event caused an outrage among abolitionists throughout the United States.

Some opposed the execution on the ground that there was doubt about Graham's guilt and that he didn't get a competent defense. Graham was seventeen when charged with the shooting of a man in the parking lot of a Houston supermarket. He was convicted on the basis of a single, disputed, eyewitness's testimony, and no physical evidence linked him to the crime. Two other witnesses, who worked at the supermarket and claimed they got a good look at the assailant, said Graham was not the killer. But these witnesses were never interviewed by Graham's court-appointed attorney and were never called to testify at the trial. Three of the jurors who voted to convict Graham later signed affidavits saying they would have voted differently had all of the evidence been available. It was argued that, given these considerations, the execution was nothing but a murder.

The debate about capital punishment is a moral disagreement. Can it be resolved? Insofar as it is rooted in disagreement about the reliability of the legal system, or about other questions whose answer can be revealed through empirical research, it might obviously help to try to settle them. But that requires some agreement over more basic moral values. For example, the considerations mentioned in the last paragraph may potentially influence people's opinions since they appeal to views that are widely shared, also among those who are in favor of the death penalty. According to these views, everyone has a right to a fair trial, and it is wrong to punish an innocent person, especially when the punishment is so severely irreversible as the death penalty. So, if we could determine the extent to which the present system in the United States fails to live up to these standards, some of the disagreement might disappear. But not all of it. For there are cases in which the disagreement goes deeper, and is due to more fundamental differences in moral outlook. Thus, many oppose capital punishment regardless of whether those being convicted are innocent and regardless of the nature of their crimes. And in such cases, a resolution is harder to achieve, or so it is often held.

In the twentieth century, disagreement emerged within Western societies over a wide range of moral issues. And anthropological research has revealed that the differences appear even more radical when we compare Western views with those of other cultures. The Yanomamö, a people who live in the rain forest in the Amazon basin, provide an example that is particularly cherished among philosophers. Their ways have been thoroughly documented by the ethnographer Napoleon Chagnon, who attributes to them a number of views that most Westerners find difficult to accept, to say the least.

Chagnon tells us that aggression plays a crucial role in Yanomamö culture. Yanomamö men cultivate and admire relentless fierceness, both in relations between villages and between the sexes. They raid rival villages, trying to kill as many men as possible and rape and kidnap their women. They practice infanticide, or did so until recently, and supposedly think it legitimate to kill one's first child on the mere ground that it is a girl. Moreover, even very insignificant "violations" by Yanomamö women (being slow in serving dinner) can lead to battering and mutilation, and even to death.[1]

Awareness of this kind of diversity has had a great impact on people's understanding of moral thinking. Not that disagreement is anything unique for the present age, of course. But it seems fair to say that the *extent* of the diversity that has been uncovered is so impressive that it seemed more than before to call for a philosophical response.

One such response was to adopt some form of *relativism*. For example, many of the pioneering anthropologists pleaded for tolerance toward other cultures; a tolerance that seemed desperately necessary in view of the countless atrocities that have been performed in the name of the alleged cultural superiority of Western societies. This in turn led some of them

---

1  See his *Yanomamö: The Fierce People* (5th ed.). Fort Worth: Harcourt, 1997. (In this edition, Chagnon mentions that he has stopped publishing on Yanomamö infanticide, apparently for political reasons. So, for this information, see one of the early editions.) Notice also that Chagnon's views and methods have received much criticism. See, for example, Patrick Tierney's *Darkness in El Dorado: How Scientists and Journalists Devastated the Amazon*. London and New York: W.W. Norton & Company, 2000.

to endorse a view according to which norms and values are binding only for members of the cultures in which they have emerged, or are widely accepted, and that others should simply keep out.[2]

This type of relativism is best construed as a substantive ethical view. It says something about what we may and may not do. Other responses to the diversity are *meta*-ethical. They concern the nature of our moral convictions rather than which particular convictions we should adopt. Thus, recognition of the diversity has contributed to the popularity of so-called expressivist or noncognitivist views. According to these views, to think that the death penalty should be abolished is to dislike or have a negative emotional attitude (a "con-attitude") toward the death penalty, rather than a true or false belief about it.

The latter type of response rests on the thought that moral diversity is difficult to reconcile with a "realist" or "objectivist" view on ethics. That is, the diversity is supposed to be difficult to reconcile with the idea that moral issues are issues over matters of fact, issues that allow for objectively and uniquely true answers. After all, if there is an objective truth about the legitimacy of the death penalty, why can't people reach agreement over it?

But it is far from obvious, of course, that antirealism *is* the proper response to the diversity. Realists usually point out that there is disagreement also in areas where people are less prone to skepticism toward an objective truth, such as the natural sciences. What is it about *moral* diversity that motivates skepticism about objectivity in the case of ethics? Questions such as these provide the point of departure of this essay. Simply put, its aim is to discuss what moral disagreement can teach us about the nature of moral thinking.

The philosophical literature about moral disagreement is immense. It begins, perhaps, with Sextus Empiricus, who appeals to moral disagreement in support of what seems to be an antirealist view:

Things which some think bad others pursue as good – for example, indulgence, injustice, avarice, lack of self-control and the like. Hence, if things which are so and so by nature naturally affect everyone in the same way, while so-called bad things do not affect everyone in the same way, nothing is by nature bad.[3]

---

2  See, for example, Melville Herskovits's *Cultural Anthropology*. New York: Knopf, 1955. For a thorough and interesting recent discussion of Herskovits's views, see J. Cook, *Morality and Cultural Differences*. New York: Oxford University Press, 1999.

3  *Outlines of Scepticism*, sections xxiii–xxiv in Book III (§190). See Julia Annas's and Jonathan Barnes's edition (Cambridge: Cambridge University Press, 1994). For another, more recent,

Numerous articles and books follow Sextus's treatise. Still, in my view, work remains to be done. The step from disagreement to antirealism is too often supposed to be a quick and easy one, and the details are seldom scrutinized. In this book, I try to fill this gap and to set the stage for a more systematic examination of the phenomenon of moral disagreement. Notice, however, that I shall exclusively be concerned with its meta-ethical significance. Substantive ethical questions, or questions about how to live together in spite of the disagreements that plague (and enliven!) our societies, are, though interesting, of mere indirect relevance.

A discussion of the meta-ethical significance of moral disagreement could be organized in different ways. I have chosen to focus on the anti-realist arguments that take such disagreement as their point of departure. One reason is that it is in that context it usually comes up. Moreover, these arguments are, though related, really quite different. An examination of them highlights different aspects of the theories they are supposed to support or undermine, and also of the issues those theories address.

The main conclusion of this essay is that considerations that have to do with moral disagreement do indeed refute moral realism. However, as an equally important result, I count certain suggestions about the *framework* in which moral disagreement should be discussed, and about what is, or should be, at stake in the controversies around which current meta-ethics revolves.

These suggestions address issues that, in my view, are sadly neglected in contemporary meta-ethics. Much time and energy is devoted to for-mulating arguments that evoke various types of intuitions, but little to reflection upon *why* those intuitions are relevant. Pondering the latter question requires thinking about the *contents* of the theories or positions that provide the focus of meta-ethics. How could a theory such as moral realism or expressivism be vindicated? What evidence is such a theory responsive to? What are they *about*? These questions will be at the fore-front in this essay.

Throughout the book I shall use the term "moral realism" to refer to the position that provides the target of the arguments that appeal to moral disagreement. As I indicated earlier, I take it to entail that moral issues allow for objectively and uniquely correct answers. However, defining moral realism in more detail is a less easy task than one might expect,

classic in which disagreement is taken to support antirealism, see Edward Westermarck's *Ethical Relativity*. New York: Harcourt, Brace and Company, 1932.

partly as it involves addressing the methodological issues to which I have just alluded. In any case, this is the aim of Chapter 1.

In the literature about moral disagreement one often meets the locution "*the* argument from moral disagreement," as if there is only one such argument. That is false and misleading. There are several arguments (or versions of the argument) that appeal to moral disagreement; arguments that take quite different routes to their antirealist conclusions. In particular, I shall distinguish between three different arguments (or versions).

The first argument relies on premises whose truth must be established empirically. More specifically, it claims that the best explanation of the existing moral diversity entails that there are no objective moral truths. The alleged reason is that many moral disagreements are difficult if not impossible to resolve through rational means. True, in the case of other areas we don't normally think that the mere fact that people disagree provides a reason to doubt that there is a correct answer to the question over which they disagree ("Who shot JFK?"). Of course, the fact that there is disagreement entails that someone is in error. But that can usually be explained by lack of evidence, or by stubbornness or bias or some similar factor. In the case of many moral disagreements, by contrast, explanations of that kind often seem out of place. The disagreements would persist, it is held, even if the parties were cured of their irrationalities. This is why they justify our dropping the natural assumption that there is a fact of the matter regarding the issue over which they disagree.

There are basically two ways to respond to arguments of this type. One is to question the premise – the claim that actual moral disagreements really *are* deeper and more radical than disagreements in other areas. The sense in which moral diversity is supposed to be more radical is that many moral disagreements cannot be attributed to cognitive shortcomings, such as ignorance of relevant nonmoral facts, or bias or fallacious reasoning. However, it has been argued that antirealists reach this conclusion only because there are types of cognitive shortcomings that they have ignored. A closer look at the alleged examples will show that they too can be explained away. Another response to the argument, however, is to argue that, even if true, the premise still doesn't support antirealism, since the best explanation of why people disagree radically over moral issues is neither here nor there relative to the debate about realism and antirealism. Chapter 2 is devoted to the first of these responses, whereas Chapter 3 is devoted to the second.

The first argument appeals to assumptions about the *existing* moral diversity. However, it is sometimes held that the mere *possibility* of radical moral disagreement is enough to refute moral realism. For example, this is the upshot of an argument that has been put forward by Crispin Wright.[4]

Consider the claim that the best explanation of why people disagree over moral issues is that those issues have no objectively true answers. The idea is that if there *had* been such truths, we would have reason to expect convergence on them, at least in the long run and among competent inquirers. Why? Presumably, the answer is epistemological. If there had been moral truths, competent inquirers would have tracked them down. However, this is a plausible assumption only if the postulated facts are *detectable*. So a realist may resist the argument by denying that moral facts are thus detectable and insist instead that they may, as Crispin Wright puts it, "transcend, even in principle, our abilities of recognition."[5] Indeed, according to Wright, this is not merely an optional but a *mandatory* move for the realist: In the face of the mere possibility of radical moral disagreement, he *must* argue that moral facts are undetectable. And even if such a move might be plausible in other areas, it is absurd in ethics, or so it is held. It is as absurd as saying that the truth of whether someone is funny (e.g., Al Gore) also could evade even the most careful inquirer. This argument is called "the argument from epistemic inaccessibility," and will be discussed in Chapter 4.

By contrast, the argument that is examined in Chapter 5 aims to show, not that realists must conceive of moral facts as undetectable, but that they must construe some moral disagreements as *merely verbal*. This is a type of response to disagreement that may be applicable also in other areas. Why can't philosophers reach agreement over the nature of knowledge and epistemic justification? For example, "coherentists" stress that a belief is justified if it coheres with the rest of the agent's beliefs, even if they are false, whereas "reliabilists" insist that justified beliefs must be formed in accordance with a process that generates beliefs most of which are in fact true. Why can't they resolve their disagreement, in spite of being familiar with each other's moves and arguments? Perhaps as the parties to the debate really focus on different concepts of epistemic justification? Similarly, maybe the parties to a disagreement about what is morally right have different concepts of moral rightness.

---

4 See his influential *Truth and Objectivity*. Cambridge, MA: Harvard University Press, 1992, esp. Chapters 3 and 4, and "Truth in Ethics," in B. Hooker (ed.), *Truth in Ethics*, Oxford: Blackwell, 1996, 1–18.
5 *Truth and Objectivity*, 8f.

More specifically, the idea is that certain facts about our way of using ethical terms such as "morally right," "just," and so on, show that, insofar as these terms refer at all, they refer to different properties for different speakers. This in turn implies that, if two persons disagree over the application of "right" in a particular case, there need be no proposition whose truth they disagree about. But if there is no such proposition, a realist is committed to regarding the disagreement as merely apparent. And that is surely the wrong conclusion, according to the advocates of this argument.[6] I shall call it "the argument from ambiguity."[7]

In my view, it is the argument from ambiguity that provides the key. If realists were able to handle this argument, the others would provide no problem. However, I also shall argue that, as there is no believable response to the argument from ambiguity, we should reject realism.

In my view, there is a deep explanation of why the argument from ambiguity succeeds; an explanation that invokes certain views about when, and on what basis, it is legitimate to attribute moral convictions to other thinkers. After all, it is what we think about this – about what counts as a moral conviction – that ultimately determines how much disagreement we'll find in the world. It is just like any other phenomenon. Thus, consider religions. Many early anthropologists had a quite narrow concept of a religion, much narrower than the concepts that are used today. For example, it was sometimes assumed that a religion must involve the belief that there is a god who is the (omnipotent) creator of the universe. Equipped with such a notion, they found fewer religions than those we acknowledge to exist today. The same holds in the case of moralities. The stricter demands we impose, the less diversity we'll find.

A central theme in this essay is that questions about the attribution of moral judgments are of crucial relevance to the assessment of arguments that appeal to moral disagreement. And a central question is whether we can settle such issues *before* we make up our minds about the realism/antirealism debate. Indeed, why should we accept one view about when moral convictions can be correctly attributed rather than another? This question is addressed in Chapter 6.

---

6  Simon Blackburn, Richard Hare, and Charles Stevenson have all defended versions of this argument. See Blackburn, *Spreading the Word*. Oxford: Clarendon Press, 1984, 168; Hare, *The Language of Morals*. Oxford: Clarendon Press, 1952, 148ff; and Stevenson, *Facts and Values*. New Haven, CT: Yale University Press, 1963, 48–51.

7  There is another possible response to moral diversity, namely, that moral concepts are *vague*, and that seemingly irresolvable disputes concern borderline cases. I shall touch upon that suggestion at different places in this essay.

In particular, I shall focus on one thesis. Some stress that we can correctly attribute a specific belief to a person about a certain area, whether or not we share it, only if we also may attribute many beliefs about that area that we *do* share. This shared background is necessary to ensure that we talk about the same thing or subject matter. For example, suppose that someone with whom we discuss schizophrenia suddenly says that, in order to be schizophrenic, you merely need a college degree. Such exotic remarks would undermine our initial belief that we are talking about the same phenomenon.[8]

It is commonly held that there are limitations of this kind also in the moral case. Thus, Philippa Foot has famously suggested that not just any consideration could be used to back up a moral judgment: "[I]t would not do to suppose that, for instance, someone might have a *morality* in which the ultimate principle was that it was wrong to round trees right handed or to look at hedgehogs in the light of the moon."[9] Similarly, many philosophers agree with Michael Smith in thinking that it is legitimate to attribute to someone the view that an action is morally right only if he, in reaching such a verdict, is disposed to assign at least *some* relevance to facts about its consequences for the well-being of others.[10]

However, according to an idea that is central in this essay, in the case of moral convictions, it is legitimate to allow for greater "latitude" in this respect than in other areas. That is, we require *less* background agreement and tolerate more differences and idiosyncrasy in the moral case than in the case of other subject matters. I shall call the idea just indicated "the latitude idea," and I shall argue that it has a crucial role in the assessment of all of the arguments that provide the focus of this book. Indeed, I shall try to show that considerations that emerge from the discussion indicate both that we should accept the latitude idea, and that it cannot be reconciled with realism. In fact, in my view, it is the latitude idea that provides the contrast between ethics and subject matters that should be construed realistically. And this is the main lesson from disagreement for the debate about the nature of moral thinking. Or so I hold.

The major part of the work that has led to this book has been pursued at the Department of Philosophy, Stockholm University, Sweden, whose

---

8   This view is held by, among others, Donald Davidson. See, for example, *Inquiries into Truth and Interpretation*. Oxford: Clarendon Press, 1984, 168.

9   *Virtues and Vices*. Oxford: Blackwell, 1978, xii. See also essays 7 and 8.

10  See *The Moral Problem*. Oxford: Blackwell, 1994, 40f.

support I gratefully acknowledge. Part of the work also has been pursued in the context of a research project entitled "Relativism," which is funded by the Swedish Tercentenary Foundation, and led by Dag Westerståhl. Moreover, at a very important point in the process of writing the book, I got the opportunity to spend some months as a Visiting Fellow at the RSSS, Australian National University, which constitutes a context that is extraordinarily fruitful and conducive to research.

In these different contexts, I have received helpful comments from a large number of different people too numerous to enumerate. Some of the names that come to mind are Gustaf Arrhenius, Gunnar Björnsson, Ragnar Francén, Hans Mathlein, Peter Pagin, Philip Pettit, Michael Ridge, Håkan Salwén, Michael Smith, and Torbjörn Tännsjö, not to mention all my students, who have taught me the true meaning of the word "disagreement." However, I am especially indebted to two persons. One is my former supervisor, and later colleague, Lars Bergström. The second is Paisley Livingston, who has given me valuable advice in many different matters regarding the production of the book.

Parts of the book have been presented at various conferences and other universities, including the British Society for Ethical Theory Conference 2000, the Department of Philosophy, Edinburgh University; the Oxford Center for Ethics and Philosophy of Law, Oxford University; the Philosophical Institute of the Czech Academy of Sciences, Prague, Czech Republic; the Department of Philosophy, University of Copenhagen, Denmark; and the Department of Philosophy, University of Lund. I am very grateful to the audiences at these events, and in particular to John Broome, Krister Bykvist, Richard Holton, Magnus Jiborn, Toni Rönnov-Rasmussen, Barry Smith, Rae Langton, Bjorn Ramberg, Timothy Williamson, and Wlodek Rabinowicz. I am also much indebted to two anonymous referees of Cambridge University Press, whose detailed and elaborate comments have greatly improved the book. I dedicate it to my children, Hugo, Maja, and Agnes, the best philosophers I know.

# 1

## *Realism and Irrealism*

### 1.1. INTRODUCTION

It is surely an understatement to say that most of the issues that are discussed within meta-ethics appear esoteric to nonphilosophers. Still, many can relate to the questions that, in my view, provide its core, namely those that concern the *objectivity* of ethics. Can our moral commitments be valid or true? If so, can they be valid in some sense independently of *us*, for example, of the contingent fact that we accept them?

Why care about these things? Many try to live by their moral views. Some even die (or kill) for them. Behind the interest in questions about the objectivity of ethics lies the nagging suspicion that unless there is room for some objectivity, the role of moral thinking in our lives is somehow inapt. What's the point of making sacrifices in order to abide by rules whose claims to objective authority are as unfounded as any others? What's the point of carefully weighing arguments for and against moral opinions if no truth is to be found?

Of course, it is not evident that the lack of objectivity in ethics (whatever that may mean, more specifically) really does motivate taking a more casual attitude towards it. But the potential significance of such questions in that context helps to explain why nonphilosophers may find them more important than other meta-ethical questions. It also provides a perspective from which the arguments that are discussed in this book can be seen. For the point of these arguments is precisely to show that there is no room for objectivity in ethics.

However, "objective" is a tricky term, and in order to assess the arguments, we need to clarify the *sense* in which the objectivity of ethics is supposed to be undermined. That is, we need to identify the *target* of the arguments. As I mentioned in the Preface, I shall call the target "moral realism." The purpose of this chapter is to define moral realism, in part by contrasting it with its competitors. This will lead me to pursue a more general discussion about the methodological status of meta-ethical theories, a discussion that will affect the conclusions reached in subsequent chapters.

## 1.2. A DISINTEGRATED PICTURE

Fifty or so years ago, it was easy to characterize the positions that dominated meta-ethics. On the one hand, we had "noncognitivists," who denied that sentences such as "The death penalty should be abolished," and "It is right to give to charity" are true or false. On their view, to embrace such a sentence is to have a "conative" attitude toward the thing being evaluated, rather than to accept some statement of fact about it.[1]

On the other hand, we had "cognitivists" or "descriptivists", who thought that ethical sentences do express statements of fact, and that they are true or false.[2] Of course, different cognitivists differed about the *contents* of the beliefs that ethical sentences are supposed to express, just as different non-cognitivists differed about the *conative* states they are supposed to express. Some cognitivists stressed that ethical sentences represent certain "natural" states of affairs, whereas others held that the properties ascribed by ethical sentences are "nonnatural."[3] Similarly, some noncognitivists thought that ethical sentences express certain sentiments or emotions, whereas others held that they rather express a kind of command.[4]

---

1   Alfred Ayer, Richard Hare, and, more recently, Allan Gibbard are prominent advocates of this view. See A. Ayer, *Language, Truth and Logic*, Harmondsworth: Penguin, 1936 (Ch. 6); A. Gibbard, *Wise Choices, Apt Feelings*. Oxford: Clarendon Press, 1990; and Hare, *The Language of Morals*. Nowadays, this view is usually labeled "expressivism."

2   G. E. Moore and W. D. Ross are classical advocates of this view. See Moore's *Ethics*. London: Oxford University Press, 1912 and Ross's *The Right and the Good*, Oxford: Oxford University Press, 1930. For some contemporary heirs, see R. Boyd, "How to Be a Moral Realist," in G. Sayre-McCord (ed.), *Essays on Moral Realism*. Ithaca, NY: Cornell University Press, 1988, 181–228; D. O. Brink, *Moral Realism*. New York: Cambridge University Press, 1989; F. Jackson, *From Metaphysics to Ethics*. Oxford: Clarendon, 1998; and M. Smith, *The Moral Problem*.

3   "Nonnaturalism" is associated with G. E. Moore. Most contemporary cognitivists, such as Brink and Smith, regard themselves as naturalists. According to Smith, what distinguishes a "natural" property from "nonnatural" ones is that "it is of the kind that is the subject matter of a natural or social science" (*The Moral Problem*, 17).

4   Emotivism is usually attributed to Ayer and Stevenson. Richard Hare provides an example of a noncognitivist who is not an emotivist.

2

However, during the past decades, this picture has disintegrated, and it has become increasingly more difficult to discern where the opponents really differ. One step in this process was the emergence of John Mackie's "error theory." Mackie held that ethical sentences do indeed express beliefs, but, given a correct account of the contents of these beliefs, we have reason to suspect that they are all false.[5] According to Mackie, to hold that an action is, say, right is to ascribe a property that is "objectively prescriptive"; that is, such that grasping that an action has it necessarily involves being motivated to perform the action. And such properties simply do not exist.[6]

Mackie's theory is not popular. Many think it awkward to say that there is something globally wrong with ethics, given its crucial role in people's lives. In particular, many think it strange to deny that some ways of pursuing moral thinking are better or more reliable than others; a denial they think follows from Mackie's theory.[7] However, the emergence of Mackie's position carried an important lesson. It made clear that moral realism involves two components, and that a person can, accordingly, be an antirealist in two ways. We can either deny its "semantical" component (roughly, the view that moral convictions are beliefs), or its "ontological" component (the view that there are facts in virtue of which some such beliefs are true).

The emergence of Mackie's theory added a new position, but it didn't confuse the old picture. A more important step in the disintegration was the interest in so-called deflationary or minimal theories of truth.

Noncognitivism is often taken to deny that ethical sentences have truth-values. According to a "deflationary" view, however, to ascribe truth to a sentence is merely a way expressing one's agreement with it, and not (to use a phrase by Crispin Wright) "to ascribe a property of intrinsic metaphysical *gravitas*."[8] This view seems to allow a noncognitivist to concede that sentences such as "The death penalty should be abolished" may be

---

5  This holds at least for all "positive" judgments; that is, judgments that actually ascribe some moral property.
6  See Mackie's *Ethics: Inventing Right and Wrong*. New York: Penguin, 1977, Ch. 1. For an interesting recent elaboration of this type of approach, see Richard Joyce's *The Myth of Morality*. New York: Cambridge University Press, 2001.
7  For example, this is suggested by Crispin Wright. See his "Truth in Ethics," esp. 2f. See also Simon Blackburn's "Errors and the Phenomenology of Values," reprinted in *Essays in Quasi-Realism*. New York: Oxford University Press, 1993, 149–165.
8  See Crispin Wright's "Truth in Ethics," 5. For a useful discussion of the deflationary view, see H. Field, "The Deflationary Conception of Truth," in G. MacDonald and C. Wright (eds.), *Fact, Science and Morality*. Oxford: Blackwell, 1986, 55–117.

true. For, given the deflationary view, to ascribe truth to this sentence is just to affirm it. And that is, obviously, something a noncognitivist can do.

On the basis of the present reasoning, many antirealists argue that ethical sentences are, after all, true or false. C. L. Stevenson, Jack Smart, and, more recently, Simon Blackburn and Wright himself, provide prominent examples.[9] For example, Blackburn stresses that

> [t]o think [. . .] that the anti-realist results show that there is no such thing as moral truth is quite wrong. To think there are no moral truths is to think that nothing should be morally endorsed, that is, to endorse the endorsement of nothing, and this attitude of indifference is one that it would be wrong to recommend, and silly to practice.[10]

Indeed, Blackburn holds that this strategy allows an antirealist to hold not only that ethical sentences may be true, but also that there are moral facts, that those facts exist independently of us, that we can obtain knowledge of them, and so forth. This is the idea underlying his "quasi-realism."[11]

What remains, then, of the antirealism of these writers? Stevenson stresses that the fact that a sentence can be true shows "nothing whatsoever about whether it expresses a belief or an attitude."[12] Given this view, one may accept that ethical sentences have truth-values, but deny that they express beliefs, which is exactly what Stevenson does. Blackburn and Wright formulate themselves differently, but they pursue what is basically the same strategy. Thus, Blackburn insists that we may separate "truth [. . .] from 'represents' and its allies," and argues that, insofar as ethical sentences express beliefs, these beliefs do not have "representational truth conditions thought of realistically."[13] Similarly, Wright suggests that, although the claim that ethical sentences are truth apt commits him to the view that they express beliefs, these beliefs are not "full-bloodedly representational."[14]

---

9  See, for example, Blackburn, *Spreading the Word*, 196; Stevenson, *Facts and Values*, 216; J.J.C. Smart, *Ethics, Persuasion and Truth*. London: Routledge & Kegan Paul, 1984, 97; and Wright, *Truth and Objectivity*, 89.

10  "Moral Realism," in J. Casey (ed.), *Morality and Moral Reasoning*. London: Methuen, 1971, 101–124.

11  *Essays in Quasi-Realism*, 3–11. Roughly, "quasi-realism" is the project of explaining how an antirealist may legitimately talk about moral facts and knowledge.

12  *Facts and Values*, 216. Smart holds a similar view. See *Ethics, Persuasion and Truth*, 94–105.

13  See "Attitudes and Contents," reprinted in *Essays in Quasi-Realism*, 182–197, 185. See also *Spreading the Word*, 167, in which he says that ethical sentences lack "genuine truth conditions."

14  See, for example, his *Truth and Objectivity*, 91f and 162. See also "Realism: Pure and Simple?," *International Journal of Philosophical Studies* 2 (1994), 327–341, in which Wright says that the

In suggesting that some beliefs, unlike others, are "full-bloodedly representational," Blackburn and Wright assume that beliefs may differ in the "way" or "sense" in which they may be true. Some represent, unlike others, "robust" facts. It may be questioned whether a clear sense could be attached to idea, and I shall return to that issue. But it also might be wondered why antirealists want to adopt the view that ethical sentences are truth apt in the first place.

One reason is that this enables them to account for certain "objectivist" features of ethical discourse. For example, it is commonly assumed that ethical sentences occur in logically valid inferences, and that they can be inconsistent with each other. It is also held that we should avoid such inconsistencies. If we assume that ethical sentences are truth apt, we may offer a straightforward account both of what it means to say that ethical sentences are inconsistent, and of why we should avoid accepting inconsistencies among our moral convictions. According to this account, a set of sentences is inconsistent if it is necessarily so that one of them is false, and we should avoid inconsistencies because we want to avoid error. If ethical sentences are not truth apt, however, our explanation of these things may have to be complicated.[15]

A similar attempt to occupy the ground of its rival can be discerned in the realist camp. It is commonly recognized that we have a (defeasible) tendency to act in accordance with our moral judgments. For example, if someone thinks it immoral to eat meat, we would be surprised (and not merely annoyed) if we were to find that he lacks a tendency to avoid meat. This correlation provides the point of departure of a traditional objection to moral realism. For the correlation is often taken to support *internalism*, and that position is often supposed to be difficult to reconcile with realism.

status he ascribes to ethical sentences is related to that which he ascribes to vague sentences (although it stems from a different source). Notice that Blackburn's and Wright's antirealisms differ substantially. Blackburn is an expressivist who regards himself as an heir of Ayer and Hare. For an account of Wright's antirealism, see his "Truth in Ethics".

15  I allude here to what is often called "the Frege-Geach problem." See P. T. Geach, "Assertion," *Philosophical Review* 74 (1965), 449–465; and G. F. Scheuler, "Modus Ponens and Moral Realism," *Ethics* 98 (1988), 492–500. That this provides the main reason to accept that ethical sentences are truth apt is stressed by Crispin Wright. See his "Truth in Ethics," 3f. I shall not enter into the huge discussion about whether expressivists can account for the Frege-Geach considerations, as my aim in this essay is not to defend expressivism but to discuss realism, which is a stronger thesis than that which the Frege-Geach considerations are taken to support.

The reason is this. Internalism tells us that to judge that an action is right necessarily involves being motivated to perform it (the motivation is "internal" to the judgment).[16] Realists hold that such judgments are best construed as a kind of belief. However, given a popular view about human psychology (that is commonly attributed to Hume), it holds for any belief that it is possible to have that belief and still not be motivated to perform any particular action (due to the absence of appropriate desires). Therefore, given the "Humean" view, internalism is difficult to reconcile with realism.[17]

Some realists respond to this argument by denying internalism (at least in the form considered here) and by trying to explain the correlation between evaluation and motivation in a way that is compatible with internalism being false (e.g., by assuming that we have an independently existing desire to do the right thing).[18] Others question instead the psychological theory on which it relies. For example, John McDowell and David Wiggins think that some beliefs are necessarily motivating, which allows them to combine the claim that judging that giving to charity is right is to have a belief (cognitivism), with the doctrine that making the judgment necessarily involves a tendency to give to charity (internalism).[19]

What all of this shows is in any case that, just as there is in politics a rush toward the center, so is there a similar rush toward the center in meta-ethics. And, just as in politics, it may be difficult to see where the real frontiers lie. In my view, although some of the old ways of stating the debates might be misleading in view of new developments, substantial disagreements remain. The rest of this chapter is an attempt to pin them down.

16  For some discussions of internalism, see W. D. Falk, "'Ought' and 'Motivation'," *Proceedings of the Aristotelian Society*, 48 (1947–8), 492–510; W. Frankena, "Obligation and Motivation in Recent Moral Philosophy," in A. Melden (ed.), *Essays in Moral Philosophy*. Seattle: University of Washington Press, 1958, 40–81; Brink, *Moral Realism*; and Smith, *The Moral Problem*, 60–91.

17  To reconcile internalism with realism, without giving up the Humean view of psychology is, roughly, what Michael Smith labels "the moral problem." See *The Moral Problem*, Ch. 1.

18  This view is labeled "externalist," because, in this view, our motivation to act in accordance with our moral judgments is "external" to the judgments. David Brink and Richard Boyd are two advocates of this view. See Brink, *Moral Realism*, and Boyd, "How To Be a Moral Realist."

19  See McDowell's "Are Moral Requirements Hypothetical Imperatives?," *Proceedings of the Aristotelian Society* 52 (suppl.), 1978, 13–29; "Values and Secondary Qualities," in T. Honderich (ed.), *Morality and Objectivity*. London: Routledge & Kegan Paul, 1985, 110–129; and Wiggins' "Truth, Invention and the Meaning of Life," in his *Needs, Values, Truth*, Oxford: Blackwell, 1987, 87–138. See also J. Dancy, *Moral Reasons*. Oxford: Blackwell, 1993, Ch. 1. For an able defense of the Humean theory, see Smith, *The Moral Problem*, Ch. 4.

To make a long story short, I shall conceive of moral realism as the conjunction of four claims: *cognitivism, antinihilism, absolutism* (antirelativism), and *objectivism*. I shall comment on these components in turn, but I shall especially focus on the first.

Cognitivism and its competitors are often stated in terms of the *words* or *sentences* we use for expressing our moral convictions. In my view, this is a dubious approach. But as the considerations that show why carry some important lessons, it is worth our while to spend some pages on it.

Cognitivism is usually taken to involve the following claim:

(1) Ethical sentences express beliefs.[20]

(1) in turn is closely related to a number of other claims usually associated with cognitivism, such as the thesis that ethical sentences have truth conditions and are true or false, that they have "cognitive content," that ethical terms such as "right," "wrong," etc., refer to "real properties," and so on. These claims are sometimes supposed to follow from (1), and are sometimes supposed to imply (1).[21]

However, in my view, (1) does a bad job at capturing cognitivism, at least if we want to define the position in such a way that those who regard themselves as noncognitivists really deny it, and in a way that makes sense of the arguments around which the debate revolves. What is a sentence, and which sentences are ethical ? A sentence is a (well-formed) sequence of words, characters or phonemes, and it is customary to distinguish ethical sentences from others by stressing that they contain words such as "obligatory," "morally wrong," and "unjust" (e.g., "It is morally wrong to $X$").[22] The problem is that, more or less regardless of what we mean by "express beliefs," it is hard to see how anyone can deny (1).

This has in part to do with the fact that language is so context-sensitive. Roughly, to have a belief is to hold a certain proposition $p$ to be true.[23] On one (admittedly vague) suggestion, to say that a sentence expresses the

---

20 Of course, it sounds wrong to say that sentences express something by themselves. Rather, it is *we* who express beliefs, by using sentences. This should be kept in mind in what follows.

21 For example, Frank Jackson and Philip Pettit think that (1) entails that ethical sentences have truth conditions. See their "A Problem for Expressivism," *Analysis* 58 (1998), 239–251.

22 I use "ethical" and "moral" interchangeably throughout the book, although I often reserve "ethical" for linguistic expressions and "moral" for the kinds of commitments they are used to express.

23 The notion of a proposition is problematic in certain well-known ways. However, these problems have no bearing on the present context.

belief that $p$ is to say that, by uttering the sentence, a speaker represents himself as having the belief that $p$.[24] That there are contexts in which terms such as "morally wrong" are used to express beliefs in this sense is clear enough. For example, consider the sentence "It is morally wrong for Mormons to have premarital sex," and suppose that it is uttered as an answer to the following question: "What do Mormons think about sex and marriage?" In that context, the sentence should obviously be interpreted as conveying information about what Mormons *think* is right rather than as expressing a judgment about what *is* right (for Mormons). In other words, as Richard Hare and others have put it, ethical terms are sometimes used in an "inverted commas sense."[25]

One way to handle this familiar problem is to restrict (1) to certain contexts, namely, those that are "typically moral." In that way, the fact that ethical sentences express beliefs in *other* contexts (e.g., when they are used in an inverted commas sense) is irrelevant. But a further problem is that, however we pick those contexts out, noncognitivists typically hold that ethical sentences express beliefs in them as well.

This holds most clearly for "thick" sentences, such as "Socrates was courageous" (which expresses straightforward beliefs about Socrates' way of facing dangers).[26] But many noncognitivists stress that "thin" ethical terms, such as "right," also might acquire the capacity to express beliefs, even in typically moral contexts. For example, Hare suggests that such terms may acquire that capacity "by reason of the constancy of the standards by which they are applied."[27] In a similar vein, Stevenson writes that:

to say that a man is 'good' may be to suggest that he has such traits as honesty, humility [. . .], and so on. [. . .] Within communities with well-developed mores these varied suggestions become fixed, and people tend to define 'good' in a way that makes the word strictly designate what it formerly suggested.[28]

In my view, in spite of these "concessions," there is room for a distinctively noncognitivist position. This means, however, that cognitivism must be construed as stating something more than just (1).

---

24  That is, the utterance itself (provided that it is sincere) allows us to conclude that the speaker believes that $p$, even if we know nothing else about him than the fact that he speaks the language to which the sentence belongs.

25  See, for example, *The Language of Morals*, 124.

26  See, for example, Gibbard, *Wise Choices*, 113.

27  See *The Language of Morals*, 7, in which he suggests that "right" may acquire the capacity to refer to the property of maximizing utility in a society of convinced utilitarians.

28  *Facts and Values*, 169, my italics. See also 9, 16, and 221.

But what? One option is to try to exploit a distinction between "primary" and "secondary" functions. For example, Hare concedes that ethical sentences may express beliefs. But he also stresses that this is just their "secondary" function. Their "primary" function is – he thinks – to express other (i.e., conative) attitudes.[29] Cognitivism, we may assume, makes the converse claim.

But what does this talk of "primary" and "secondary" functions amount to? In the present section, I shall pursue a certain suggestion. This suggestion is not meant to capture exactly what Hare meant with such phrases, but constitutes rather a proposal as to how cognitivism *should* be defined.

One set of questions about cognitivism concern its scope. Is it supposed to hold for all languages or idiolects, at all times? Or could cognitivism be true of some languages and false of others? For example, someone might argue that while cognitivism might have been true of, say, thirteenth-century Swedish, it is false of the Swedish of this secular age. In medieval Sweden, there were recognized moral authorities (the church and its priests), and a significant amount of consensus regarding when to count actions as right or wrong. Therefore, there were shared criteria in the light of which it made sense to say that someone was correct in case of a moral dispute, which in turn, it might be held, is enough to show that the issue over which they disagreed concerned a matter of fact, and that ascriptions of "right" were true or false. In this modern age, however, the consensus has withered and the authorities have fallen into disrepute, which rather invites an expressivist analysis.

I suppose that one *could* reason in this way. But I shall pursue another idea. It is interesting to note that although both thirteenth-century and contemporary Swedish contain an ethical vocabulary, the overlap is not complete. For example, the term "god-fearing" (or its counterpart in Swedish) was once an evaluative term, and was used to express a moral evaluation of a person, but is now seldom if ever used in that way. However, the slightly different vocabularies still have something in common, and something that sets them apart from other vocabularies; that is, something that "makes" them the ethical vocabularies of the idiolects in question. What they have in common, more specifically, is the fact that speakers relate to them in certain ways. For example, they have a special role in

---

29  See, for example, *The Language of Morals*, 121–126. Simon Blackburn makes a similar suggestion in "Attitudes and Contents" (see 185).

planning and in practical decision making. Of course, which words it is that have this role in a language may change over time. This explains why a term ("god-fearing") could be an ethical term at one stage even if lacks that status at another.

Now, on one suggestion, to say that it is the "primary function" of ethical sentences to express beliefs is to say that this is what they express in virtue of the facts that "make" them ethical. What they express in virtue of *other* facts are mere "secondary" functions. In my view, this suggestion is, though vague and in need of clarification, on the right track. Moreover, it helps to explain how noncognitivists can concede that ethical sentences express beliefs.

Which facts, then, "make" sentences ethical? Following Michael Smith, we may say that they fall into two classes. On the one hand, we may talk about the "practicality" of ethical discourse, which is manifested in the fact that people have a (defeasible) tendency to act in accordance with their verdicts on ethical sentences.[30] On the other hand, there is its "objectivity," which is manifested in the fact that we develop arguments in support of our verdicts, that we try to avoid inconsistency among them, and that we acknowledge that we must be able to provide some response to the arguments submitted by our opponents, and so on.[31]

However, the considerations that "make" ethical sentences ethical do not include the kind of "constancy" Hare and Stevenson mention in connection with their observation that ethical terms may be used to express beliefs. For example, in the scenario sketched by Stevenson, ethical terms acquire the capacity to express beliefs because of the emergence of agreement about when to apply them. Thus, people have come to agree in thinking that a person is not properly called "good" unless he is honest. On some views on meaning, this is enough to show that the sentence "*a* is good" has acquired the capacity to express the belief that *a* is honest. However, such agreement is not included among the features of our use of ethical sentences that make them ethical. The reason is that, if it were to evaporate, this would not mean that the sentences would no longer be ethical. It would just mean that people's moral views have changed.[32] So, the existence of agreement concerning how to apply ethical terms shows at best that it is a *secondary* function of ethical sentences to express beliefs.

---

30  Notice that this feature should not be construed so as to presuppose internalism; that is, the view that to have a moral judgment *necessarily* involves motivation.

31  See *The Moral Problem*, Ch. 1.

32  Thus, even if all ethical terms, through the emergence of agreement, would "turn thick," this would do nothing to vindicate cognitivism.

10

The present suggestion also allows us to explain why a certain kind of "slingshot" argument for cognitivism is flawed. Thus, it might be held that the mere fact that we classify actions as "good," and "right," and so on, on the basis of their (nonmoral) properties, and thus associate certain criteria with these terms (criteria that determine whether an action falls under the terms or not) is enough to show that cognitivism is true, because it shows that sentences that predicate those terms express beliefs (beliefs to the effect that the actions have the properties in question).[33] However, on the present construal of cognitivism, this reasoning is flawed. For the fact that ethical terms are used to classify items is not anything that holds *specifically* for ethical terms. Therefore, what we are entitled to infer from it is, again, irrelevant to their primary function.[34]

Notice, finally, that the present suggestion rules out the possibility that cognitivism might be true of one language but false of another. The reason is that, given this approach, we focus, not on some particular set of strings of letters, but on those features of our use of those strings in virtue of which they are ethical. And these features are common to all ethical sentences, regardless of what language they belong to.

### 1.5. BELIEFS AND DESIRES

Still, the above account leaves many questions unanswered. In particular, one has to clarify what it means for a sentence to express beliefs "in virtue of" the considerations that make it ethical. However, I shall sidestep all those problems. For there is a simpler way to state much of what has just been said. What this account illustrates is that the sentences we use to express our moral commitments are of little interest in themselves. It is the commitments *themselves* that are interesting. That is, cognitivism and expressivism are, on the present suggestion, theories about the nature of these commitments. What is it to answer a moral question and to think that an action is right or wrong? Is it to form a belief or a conative attitude of some sort, such as a desire? Cognitivists believe the former,

---

33 Such an argument is suggested by Donald Davidson in his "Objectivity and Practical Reason," in E. Ullman-Margalit (ed.), *Reasoning Practically*. Oxford: Oxford University Press, 2000, 17–26, see esp. p. 19.

34 It might be argued that the fact that expressivists can concede that ethical sentences (secondarily) express beliefs also enables them to accommodate the claim that they can be true and false, and, in effect, respond to the Frege-Geach problem. For, according to a common view, a sentence has a truth-value in virtue of the belief it is used by speakers to express. So, once we recognize that expressivists can concede that ethical sentences express beliefs (for some speakers and in some contexts), we also see that they can accept that ethical sentences have truth-values and thus employ the traditional notion of validity in explaining the fact that (for those speakers, and in those contexts) those sentences stand in logical relations to others.

while expressivists hold the latter. And an expressivist can add that the fact that ethical sentences sometimes express beliefs shows just that ethical sentences are not *only* used to express our answers to moral issues.

I shall call the relevant commitments "moral judgments" or "moral convictions."[35] The central claim of cognitivism may thus be formulated:

(C) Moral judgments consist (solely) of beliefs.

And expressivism can be stated:

(E) Moral judgments consist (solely) of certain conative states.[36]

However, just like (1), these claims raise many questions. For example, it is an oft-noted fact that "belief," is ambiguous. On the one hand, it could refer to a psychological state (as when we say that beliefs are dispositions to act). On the other hand, it rather refers to something that might represent the *content* of such a state (as when we say that "all those beliefs are false," thereby denying a certain set of propositions, regardless of whether they are in fact believed by anyone). So, what notion does (C) assume? I shall assume that it is the first: "beliefs" (and accordingly "moral judgments") should, be interpreted as referring to a kind of psychological state.[37]

But what *is* a belief, construed in this way, and what distinguishes beliefs from the conative states expressivists think moral judgments consist in? The view that there is a crucial contrast between beliefs and, for example, desires is central in many accounts of intentional behavior, and I shall more or less take it as primitive. I shall assume that one aspect of the difference is that beliefs, unlike desires, are true or false.[38] Beyond this, however, I shall not say much. Let me explain why.

---

35  Notice that, throughout the essay, I use "moral judgments" and "moral convictions" as synonyms. The term "judgments" may seem biased in favor of cognitivism. However, the idea is, of course, that it is an open question whether moral judgments are beliefs or, say, desires. For a usage similar to mine, see S. Darwall, A. Gibbard, and P. Railton, "Toward *Fin de siècle* Ethics," *Philosophical Review* 101 (1992) 115–189, in which it is said that expressivists "explain moral language as expressing moral judgments, and explain moral judgments as something other than beliefs" (148f).

36  Of course, besides these "pure" theories, we may imagine "hybrid" ones, according to which moral convictions consist of mixtures of beliefs and desires. The theory suggested by David Copp in his "Realist-Expressivism: A Neglected Option for Moral Realism," *Social Philosophy and Policy* 18 (2001), 1–43, provides an interesting example of a theory that combines cognitivist and expressivist elements.

37  Do moral judgments have contents and, if so, in what do they consist? If they consist in beliefs, the answer is straightforward: Like (other) beliefs they do have contents, and their contents consist in propositions. However, in an expressivist setting the question is more complex.

38  Could psychological *states* be true or false? This may sound strange, almost like saying that drops of water could be true or false. However, beliefs may be true or false, just like sentences (and unlike drops of water), because they have propositional contents.

I agree with the common view that beliefs and desires are best conceived of as dispositions to act. The fact that a person *a* has such a disposition, moreover, means that certain counterfactuals are true of *a*. Maybe the difference between believing and desiring could be explicated in terms of *which* these counterfactuals are?

This is the upshot of a suggestion made by Michael Smith. According to Smith, to believe that *p* is to be in a state such that, if one were to perceive that not-*p*, it would tend to go out of existence. To *desire* that *p*, by contrast, is to be in a state that tends to endure when we perceive that not-*p*.[39]

Smith points out that this suggestion squares with the popular idea that the difference between beliefs and desires should be explained in terms of "directions of fit". Beliefs are states aimed at fitting with the world, whereas desires are states aimed rather at making the world fit with them.[40] This explains why a person who believes that *p* would react differently to the perception that not-*p* compared to a person who desires that *p*.

However, unless we already have a grasp of the distinction between beliefs and desires, Smith's proposal is not illuminating. The reason is that it invokes the concept of someone "perceiving that not-*p*." Surely, this is a cognitive state of precisely the kind whose difference from conative ones is at issue. For example, to perceive that not-*p* presumably involves believing truly that not-*p*. So, Smith's proposal presupposes that we already know the difference.

Still, surely Smith is correct in stressing that our best hope of understanding the concepts of belief and desire lies in focusing on their functional roles. Beliefs and desires are attributed to an individual in order to make sense of, and predict, his behavior, and it is from their role in this practice that those concepts derive their contents.

The fact that beliefs and desires manifest themselves in behavior may lead one to think that those concepts can be reduced to more behaviorist ones. However, for well-known reasons, there is no such viable hope. The main reason has to do with the fact that beliefs and desires are attributed holistically. If a person behaves in a certain way, this may plausibly be seen as a manifestation of a specific belief, but only *given* certain assumptions about his desires. Given other assumptions, the same behavior would justify attribution of other beliefs. In other words, there is no particular set of behavior that is tied to any specific belief, and no set

39   See Smith, *The Moral Problem*, 111–116.
40   This idea is usually attributed to Elisabeth Anscombe. See her *Intention*, Oxford: Blackwell, 1957.

of behavior that may be associated with the state of believing as contrasted with the state of desiring. This underlies the difficulties of providing an illuminating account of the difference between those states in terms of the behavior they give rise to.[41]

## 1.6. MORAL JUDGMENTS

But (C) – the claim that moral judgments consist of beliefs – raises other questions. What kind of a claim is (C)? Is it an empirical hypothesis, on a par with the claim that water consists of $H_2O$ molecules? Or should it be conceived as a kind of definition of the phrase "moral judgment"?

The first proposal faces some difficulties. It might be tempting to conceive of moral judgments as forming a natural kind, whose nature might be uncovered by carefully examining particular samples. However, this requires, presumably, that we have some independent criterion on what counts as a sample. To be sure, there may be cases over which everyone would agree. But, in other cases, the disagreement is notorious.

This is especially true of the cases over which the competing theories differ. Thus, consider the *amoralist*. According to externalists such as David Brink, we may consistently imagine persons who have no tendency to act in accordance with their moral convictions.[42] For example, we may imagine persons who attribute terms such as "right" and "just" to actions or states of affairs just like we do, and on the basis of similar considerations. This entitles us to conclude that they have moral judgments. Still, it does not exclude that they may be completely unmoved by those judgments.

Obviously, the possibility of amoralists refutes internalism (at least in the form mentioned earlier), and theories that imply it (e.g., expressivism). It is not surprising, therefore, that expressivists deny that the concept of a amoralist is a coherent one. Even if the persons imagined by externalists share *some* properties with those that make moral judgments, these similarities are, it is stressed, superficial and irrelevant. For a crucial difference remains, namely that they lack the appropriate motivation. This is why internalists think that the proper conclusion is that the (alleged) amoralists do not in fact make any genuine judgments and merely use "right" and "just" in an inverted commas sense.

---

41  The irreducibility of the concept of belief and the concept of desire is stressed by Donald Davidson. See, for example, his "Toward a Unified Theory of Meaning and Action," *Grazer Philosophische Studien* 11 (1980), 1–12.
42  See *Moral Realism*, Ch. 3.

But why is *that* the crucial difference? Doesn't this reasoning simply beg the question? In the absence of an independently justified criterion on when a difference or similarity is relevant, we seem unable to proceed beyond the kind of stalemate that, in my view, dominates the current debate.

Similar problems face the suggestion that (C) should be conceived as a definition, at least insofar as it is supposed to capture a ("the") common usage of phrases such as "moral judgments" and "moral conviction." It is often thought that we may test such definitions against our intuitions about imagined and concrete examples of people who embrace moral judgments. However, as we just noted, our intuitions come apart, even among people who have thought things through. Are we to conclude that they assign different meanings to the term "moral judgments"? Of course, this possibility cannot be ruled out beforehand, but it should in my view only be the last resort.

And there is in fact a third possibility that allows us to construe the discussion as substantial. Rather than conceiving of the debate as being about what the notion "moral judgment" does mean, we may take it to concern what it *should* mean, in order to serve certain theoretical purposes. Consequently, the debate about the possibility of an amoralist is not about whether the meaning of "moral judgment" *does* allow for such a possibility, but whether it *should* do so.

Of course, to resolve a debate through stipulation may seem unsatisfactory. But this is not stipulation just out of the tube. Consider the finding that whales are not fish. It might be tempting to see this as the result of mere stipulation. After all, it was known before that whales, unlike fish, have the characteristics that make them mammals (give birth to live young, feed them with milk, and so on). However, the revision was prompted by the fact that a concept of a fish that excludes whales is more useful in our overall theory about the species and their origins. For the animals that belong to the narrower extension have certain *other* properties in common, properties that set them apart from the rest of the animals who live in water and are assigned a special significance by the theory in question. Thus, the narrower concept can be used to state the theory in a simpler way. This is, ultimately, what justifies treating the fact that whales give birth to live young, and so on, as crucial differences. My contention is that internalism about moral judgments is to be justified in a similar way.

What the example about whales really illustrates is that the distinction between stipulations and discoveries is less clear than one might first think. It also illustrates that claims of the type we are now pondering are to be tested holistically. Consider the thesis that electrons are negatively charged. Surely, there is little hope of determining whether something is an electron *before* finding out whether it is negatively charged. Rather, the claim that electrons are negatively charged is justified, if at all, in view of how well the physical theory to which it belongs *as a whole* fits the evidence.

Could something similar be said about (C) or (E)? This is the suggestion that I propose. More specifically, I shall pursue the idea that assumptions about the nature of moral judgment have a role to play in the "theory" or framework sometimes called "folk psychology," and that they should be evaluated in that context. Of course, there is much controversy about the status and content of folk psychology. But one of its central claims is the following: among the states a person could be in there are psychological states, such as beliefs, desires, intentions, and so on, and attributions of such states help to explain, and predict, human behavior. The idea is that our moral judgments constitute a subset of these states, and that assumptions about the nature of these commitments are justified to the extent that they figure in or contribute to the best general account of human behavior.[43]

More specifically, I shall argue that meta-ethical assumptions such as (C) and (E) can be tested by seeing whether the states they pick out as moral convictions are indeed assigned a special role by an adequate general theory. Or differently put, by considering whether the behavior or phenomena attributions of those states help to explain really does motivate our introducing a special concept in the way indicated above. In particular, I shall argue along these lines in favor of "the latitude idea" that was mentioned in the Preface. That is, I shall try to show that the construal of the concept of a moral judgment which is most useful in a general account of human behavior allows for the possibility of finding that someone disagrees with you about a specific moral issue, even if that person's verdict is based on quite different considerations from those you take to be relevent, and even if his verdict cannot be blamed on some cognitive deficiency or shortcoming. Since the latitude idea in turn is a crucial premise in my main argument against moral realism, this is a central reasoning in the book. It is fully developed in Chapter 6 but foreshadowed by much of the discussion in the preceding chapters.

---

43 Notice that this is not to say that our moral judgments have to be *sui generis*. For example, according to cognitivism, moral judgments consist of beliefs. However, the talk of moral judgments as a distinct class of states may still be justified, provided that they have a special explanatory role, distinct from the role of (other) beliefs (or desires). This would justify our complicating the conceptual apparatus of the theory by introducing a term that specifically denotes this class.

So much for cognitivism. What about the other components of moral realism? Realism does not only imply that moral judgments consist of beliefs. It also implies that there are facts in virtue of which those beliefs can be true. I shall call this component "antinihilism." But there are further components.

Up to this point, I have not said much about the *contents* of the beliefs that, according to cognitivism, constitute our moral judgments. However, different cognitivists have different views about this, and it might be wondered if all of these views square with realism. For example, what about subjectivism? According to subjectivism, to think that the death penalty should be abolished is to believe that one disapproves of it. Thus, according to subjectivism, moral convictions are beliefs, and there are facts in virtue of which some of these beliefs may be true.

Does this mean that subjectivism is a version of realism? It does not. Indeed, I exclude *any* version according to which people ascribe different properties to an action by judging it right, wrong, and so on. For example, I exclude theories to the effect that moral judgments contain an implicit *indexical* element, which refers to, say, the speaker's culture or group.[44]

In other words, moral realism is conceived as an *absolutist* and *anti-relativist* position.[45] Notice that the scope of this absolutism is wide. Thus, the fact that we ascribe the same property to an action by judging it, for example, morally right is not only supposed to hold for speakers of English, but for the speakers of *any* language. And a sentence that predicates a word to an action, no matter which language the word belongs to, is an expression of that judgment only if it refers to the property in question.

---

44  This type of view is defended in Wong, *Moral Relativity*. Berkeley: University of California Press, 1984; and in G. Harman, "Moral Relativism Defended," *Philosophical Review* 84 (1975), 3–22. I shall return to Wong's views in Ch. 3.

45  For a similar view, see Richard Boyd's "How To Be a Moral Realist," 186, in which he stresses that realism is a "radically nonsubjectivist" position. See also Horgan and Timmons, "Copping Out on Moral Twin Earth," *Synthese* 124 (2000), 139–152. Paul Bloomfield has recently objected to this association of realism with absolutism in "The Rules of 'Goodness': An Essay on Moral Semantics," *American Philosophical Quarterly* 40 (2003), 197–213, esp. 200–202. Bloomfield thinks that a realist should deny absolutism on the ground that "the facts which make each person unique must be considered in figuring out what ought to be done" (201). However, this kind of agent-relativism is entirely compatible with absolutism, given the way it is construed in this book. One may consistently hold that an action is right in virtue of the particular facts of the agent and deny that, when predicating "right," different speakers refer to different properties.

One reason for this (terminological) decision is that the converse view cannot account for the realist intuition that moral issues are issues over matters of fact; issues that allow for uniquely true answers. For a relativist must concede that, although genuine moral disputes sometimes represent, or constitute, conflicts of beliefs (e.g., when the parties belong to the same culture), on other occasions they might not. For example, subjectivists hold that we can judge differently about abortion and still not disagree about the truth of any proposition (because my belief that I approve of an action is compatible with your belief that you disapprove of it). Thus, insofar as we still address the same moral issue, there is no "factual" question that this issue can be equated with. In other words, subjectivism allows for the possibility that two persons are in moral disagreement even if they do not have incompatible beliefs.[46]

Notice that the same holds for noncognitivism. To answer a moral issue is to form a moral judgment. Thus, to deny that moral judgments can be true or false is to deny that moral issues are issues over matters of fact. This is why expressivists hold that people can agree over every fact, and still fail to have settled their moral disagreements.[47] Realists, by contrast, believe that, under those conditions, no dispute remains to be resolved.

### 1.8. OBJECTIVISM

In characterizing realism, it is customary to add yet another claim, namely that moral judgments may not only be true, but "objectively" so. This is why there is supposed to be room for the kind of antirealism Crispin Wright and others advocate; the kind that concedes that ethical sentences may be true.

But what does it *mean* to say that a claim is objectively true? A common view is that a commitment is objectively true if it is true independently of the fact that people believe that it is true, or are able to show that it is true. However, that view is not very helpful in the present context.

Consider again the deflationary view on truth. According to this view, to ascribe truth to the view that, say, the death penalty should be abolished

---

46  Notice that the difference between relativism and absolutism is that relativism, unlike absolutism allows for the *possibility* that we ascribe different properties to an action by judging it right. It does not imply that we always do ascribe different properties. Thus, subjectivism would be a form of relativism even if there were only one speaker.

47  That this is an implication of expressivism is stressed by several expressivists. For example, see Blackburn, *Ruling Passions.* Oxford: Clarendon Press, 1998, 70; and Stevenson, *Ethics and Language,* 14.

is simply to affirm it. This may allow an expressivist to hold that such views can, after all, be true. Must he deny that this possible truth is objective? It seems not. For to deny that it is objective is, on the present suggestion, to hold that the wrongness of the death penalty depends on what we think, or are able to show, rather than, as, for example, a utilitarian would have it, on its consequences. But, surely, expressivists can be utilitarians.[48]

However, I take it that Wright's and Blackburn's basic idea is simply that ethics is discontinuous in important ways with discourses such as, say, physics or biology. This suggests that realism should be construed as a kind of "continuity thesis," in that it implies that moral judgments may be true and representational in the "same way" as physical claims, whatever that is. Similarly, it implies that moral properties are "as robust as" the properties ascribed in physics.[49] Geoffrey Sayre-McCord puts the point as follows. He stresses that realism must be "seamless" in the sense that "whichever theories of meaning and truth are offered for the disputed [moral] claims must be extended as well to apply to all claims."[50]

I shall construe the (admittedly vague) idea that moral judgments are not different in the indicated sense from beliefs in these other areas as a direct implication of cognitivism. On this view, Wright's form of antirealism comes out as a version of noncognitivism. I am inclined to think that the same holds for the kind of theory developed by John McDowell and David Wiggins. The reason is that McDowell and Wiggins commit themselves to the idea that moral judgments are beliefs of a special kind, in that they assume that those beliefs *in themselves* yield motivation to perform certain actions. Indeed, what McDowell and Wiggins do is really, as Michael Smith and others point out, to posit a third kind of state, distinct from both beliefs and desires ("besires").[51]

---

48  See Ronald Dworkin's article "Objectivity and Truth: You'd Better Believe It." *Philosophy & Public Affairs* 25 (1996), 87–139. Dworkin suggests that, given the most plausible interpretation of the claim that moral truths are objective, this claim has substantive ethical implications, and is defensible on purely moral grounds. Accordingly, Dworkin suggests that it is either the case that an antirealist denies a plausible moral claim or that it is not clear what he denies.

49  For suggestions along this line, see David Copp's recent "Realist-Expressivism: A Neglected Option for Moral Realism." See also Brink, *Moral Realism*, 11; P. Pettit, "Embracing Objectivity in Ethics," in B. Leiter (ed.), *Objectivity in Law and Morals*. Cambridge: Cambridge University Press, 2001, 234–286; and Wright, "Truth in Ethics," 1.

50  G. Sayre-McCord, "The Many Moral Realisms," in G. Sayre-McCord (ed.), *Essays on Moral Realism*, Ithaca, NY: Cornell University Press, 1988, 1–23, 6. This means that the central question in this essay is if the extent and nature of moral disagreement presents a *special* problem for realism about ethics.

51  See, for example, *The Moral Problem*, 119.

This is clear in view of the account of those concepts that was indicated earlier. For, given this account, an essential feature of beliefs and desires is that they are attributed holistically. That is, the fact that a person is disposed to act or behave in a certain way might be a reason for, or against, attributing some particular belief (or desire) to that person, but only given certain assumptions about the rest of his beliefs and desires. Given *other* assumptions, we may reach an entirely different conclusion on the basis of the same behavior.

This conflicts with McDowell's and Wiggins' conception of the beliefs they think constitute our moral judgments. For, in their view, the belief we express by judging an action to be morally right is such that it necessarily induces a tendency to perform this action. So, unless we have such a tendency, the belief cannot be correctly attributed to us, and there is no other consideration that can compensate for the absence of that tendency. Suppose, for example, that the belief in question *can* be correctly attributed to us at some point, because we have the relevant motivation. If we at some later point were to lose that motivation, it would be incorrect to attribute the belief to us, regardless of *other* similarities between our former and later selves. Thus, it does not matter if we still embrace the *sentence* that we, at the earlier point, used to express our belief, or are disposed to justify our verdict on it in the same way, etc. So, on the McDowell-Wiggins approach, the radical holism that I associate with beliefs does not apply to the states they equate with moral judgments.

I am inclined to think that this reasoning provides a problem for the McDowell-Wiggins theory, because we have reason to accept "the holism of the mental." And I am thus also inclined to think that it means that their theory comes out as a version of antirealism.

### 1.9. SUMMARY

In this book, then, moral realism is construed as the combination of cognitivism, antinihilism, absolutism, and objectivism. It is this position that provides the target of the arguments that I shall examine. Each of the elements may require further clarification. After all, preciseness is a matter of degrees and it is doubtful that there is a rock bottom. I just hope that I have reached a level that enables the reader to assess the arguments that are discussed in the subsequent chapters. To see if this is so, however, requires spelling out the arguments.

# 2

# *The Case for Radical Moral Disagreement*

## 2.1. INTRODUCTION

In school and through the media we have learned about all sorts of exotic practices, such as cannibalism among the Papuans of New Guinea, head shrinking among the Jivaro of Ecuador, infanticide among the Yanomamö, and senilicide among the Netsilik Eskimos. And we are all familiar with the intense debates that occur within Western societies, regarding capital punishment, euthanasia, abortion, and so on. The evidence that suggests that there is extensive moral disagreement seems overwhelming.

This partly accounts for the popularity of arguments that appeal to moral disagreement. Philosophical debates seldom can be adjudicated with reference to hard and well-established empirical facts. So when an opportunity appears to arise, it is difficult to resist the temptation.

What we must resist, however, is a simplistic view of the step from the empirical evidence to the philosophical conclusion. Disagreements occur also in areas where people are less enthusiastic about antirealism, such as in the sciences. So there has to be something peculiar about moral disagreement in order for it to serve its argumentative role. According to one idea, the contrast consists in the (alleged) fact that many moral disagreements cannot be resolved through rational argumentation. But even if there is evidence for moral diversity in general, it might be wondered if there is any evidence for this special claim as well.[1] To address that issue is the main aim of the present chapter.

---

1 Calls have been made for more research on that issue. The need for such research was aknowledged already in the 1950s by Richard Brandt, who undertook an investigation of his own of the ethics of the Hopi of the American Southwest. See his *Hopi Ethics*. Chicago:

A moral disagreement is rationally resolvable, it is often held, to the extent that it can be attributed to a cognitive shortcoming of some sort, such as ignorance of relevant nonmoral evidence, or fallacious reasoning. Let us say that disagreements that cannot be attributed to such factors are "radical." For obvious reasons, I shall not try to survey or chart all the evidence that suggests that there are radical moral disagreements. However, I shall comment on some of the evidence, and also make certain general remarks about what an empirical investigation of this issue would require.

One of the points that will be stressed is that such an investigation requires addressing a number of philosophical questions, and that this spells trouble for the idea that we in some simple way can determinate the extent to which the existing diversity is radical. For example, we need to consider which factors are to count as cognitive shortcomings, which means that we have to engage in epistemology. Moreover, and more importantly for the argumentation in this book, any report to the effect that there are moral disagreements of a certain kind ultimately relies on assumptions about when it is legitimate to attribute moral convictions to other thinkers. A problem is that the plausibility of assumptions of this kind is likely to depend on one's background meta-ethical theory. So, the question is whether we can establish such reports in a neutral way. The upshot of the chapter is that, if we turn to the phenomenon of moral disagreement in the hope of adjudicating the controversy between realism and antirealism in ethics with reference to neutral and easily accessible empirical facts, our hope is vain.

## 2.2. MORAL DISAGREEMENT

Two persons are in moral disagreement if and only if they have conflicting moral convictions. This sounds straightforward but raises in fact many questions. It is easy enough to come up with examples of moral disagreements. But how are we to conceive of them? What does it mean to have conflicting moral convictions?

It is useful to distinguish disagreements that are *genuine* from those that are merely verbal or apparent. This is illustrated by one popular realist

University of Chicago Press, 1954. For more recent pleas for empirical research, see D. Loeb, "Moral Realism and the Argument from Disagreement," *Philosophical Studies* 90 (1998), 281–303; and J. M. Doris, and S. P. Stich, "As a Matter of Fact: Empirical Perspectives on Ethics," in F. Jackson and M. Smith (eds.), *The Oxford Handbook of Contemporary Analytic Philosophy*. Oxford: Oxford University Press, forthcoming.

response to the argument from disagreement. John Mackie formulates the response as follows. Although "the actual variation of moral codes" mainly concerns derived or very specific codes, according to Mackie,

the items for which objective validity is in the first place to be claimed are not specific moral rules or codes but very general basic principles which are recognized at least implicitly in every society.[2]

For example, capital punishment is practiced in some societies but not in others. This might be because the circumstances in the relevant societies differ in such a way that the death penalty deters crime more efficiently in those where it is employed than it would in the other societies. Hence, the fact that the death penalty is used in one society but not in another does not rule out that the same basic moral principle is implicitly accepted in both societies (e.g., some form of utilitarianism).

What Mackie suggests, in effect, is that some apparent differences need not reflect a deeper disagreement, since each of the seemingly conflicting rules contains an implicit reference to a particular community. So, when a member of the first community says "The death penalty is wrong," whereas a member of the second denies this, their views need not really conflict.[3] Mackie concedes that this suggestion has some plausibility, but stresses that its scope is limited. Be that as it may, the present point is merely that it illustrates the need of a distinction between genuine disagreements and cases in which people really talk past each other.

At this point, it is useful to introduce some terminology. Let us say that an "apparent moral disagreement" is a case where an ethical *sentence* is accepted by one person and rejected by another. Such a difference could be merely apparent. For example, it is merely apparent if one of the parties (but not the other) uses the disputed sentence in an "inverted commas sense." If so, it does not provide a problem for realism. For in such a case, realists are not committed to thinking that any of the parties is in error. An apparent moral disagreement is genuine, on the other hand, if it manifests a real conflict of moral convictions.[4]

2 *Ethics*, 37.
3 Notice that we may reach this conclusion independently of what view we take on the nature of moral convictions. Thus, we should be able to make sense of the idea that a moral disagreement is merely apparent even given an expressivist or a relativist view.
4 We also may need the concept of a merely apparent *agreement*. Thus, the fact that two persons agree over the sentence "Welfare should be maximized" need not manifest any genuine agreement, as "welfare" could mean different things.

Presumably, how one conceives of such a conflict depends on one's view on the nature of moral convictions. For example, given a cognitivist view, it may seem natural to assume that we disagree morally only if we have conflicting beliefs; that is, only if the propositions that constitute the contents of our beliefs are incompatible. Given an expressivist view, we should rather explain the conflict in terms of clashing conative attitudes. For example, assuming that moral judgments constitute a form of desire, if we disagree, we have desires that cannot jointly be satisfied. Or, as C. L. Stevenson puts it: people disagree morally only

> when they have opposed attitudes to the same object [one for it and one against it] and when at least one of them has a motive for altering or calling into question the attitude of the other.[5]

Things are complicated, however, by the existence of relativist versions of cognitivism. For example, consider subjectivism. Subjectivists think that moral judgments are constituted by beliefs. Still, given subjectivism, if I think that the death penalty should be abolished and if you deny this, we need not have incompatible beliefs. For if I think that the death penalty should be abolished I believe something about me, namely, that *I* am in favor of abolition, while your denial rather concern *your* attitudes. So, given the view that we are in genuine disagreement only if we have incompatible beliefs, subjectivists seem committed to thinking that there are no (genuine) moral disagreements! Similarly, relativists who think that moral judgments contain an implicit reference to the speaker's own culture seem forced to deny that disagreements can occur between speakers of different cultures.

A relativist may avoid this conclusion by adopting the expressivist notion of a moral disagreement indicated earlier, or a "mixed" notion according to which *some* moral disagreements constitute conflicts of beliefs (e.g., when the parties belong to the same culture), whereas others do not. Realism, by contrast, entails absolutism, or so I have assumed. That is, realism entails that a sentence expresses the same moral judgment for two speakers only if the sentence expresses the same belief for both speakers (or beliefs with the same content or truth conditions). They are therefore

---

5  *Ethics and Language.* New Haven, CT: Yale University Press, 1944, 3. Allan Gibbard indicates an alternative expressivist conception in *Thinking How to Live.* Cambridge, MA: Harvard University Press, 2003, 68–75.

committed to the view that two persons are in moral disagreement only if they have conflicting beliefs.

In view of these differences, one may suspect that arguments that appeal to the existence of (genuine) moral disagreement beg the question. Is there a neutral way of determining that we face a moral disagreement? In my view, this is a crucial question, and I shall return to it a little later in this chapter. However, the mere fact that people disagree about the nature of moral disagreements does not by itself settle the issue. I conceive of the concept of a moral disagreement, just like the concept of a moral judgment itself, as a theoretical concept, introduced to explain certain phenomena. If two persons agree about the relevant phenomena, the mere fact that they have different views about the nature of a moral disagreement need not mean that they have different concepts.

Indeed, there is a way to construe a seemingly neutral notion of a genuine moral disagreement. Suppose that we are convinced that the death penalty should be abolished. One reason for thinking that someone else (say, $a$) holds the opposite view is that he rejects the sentence "Capital punishment should be abolished." However, this holds only if we can rule out the possibility that he uses the sentence in an idiosyncratic way (e.g., in an inverted commas sense). Accordingly, we may assume that, if we think that capital punishment should be abolished, $a$ disagrees with us only if there is a sentence $s$ in $a$'s idiolect such that $a$ rejects $s$, and the content of $s$ is correctly given by our sentence "Capital punishment should be abolished."[6]

All the theories that were mentioned in the preceding chapter can agree on this suggestion. In fact, it provides a convenient way to state the differences between them, namely in terms of the constraints they impose on translation manuals. Thus, consider moral realism. I have assumed that realism entails absolutism, which commits realists to the view that two persons disagree morally only if they have incompatible beliefs. Suppose that there is some sentence $s$ in $a$'s idiolect such that $s$ is rejected by $a$. If $s$ can correctly be translated with our "Capital punishment should be abolished," then $a$ disagrees with us about the morality of capital punishment. Hence, realists are committed to the idea that $s$ is correctly translated with "Capital punishment should be abolished" only if those sentences express the same beliefs in our respective idiolects (beliefs with

---

6 Notice that this conception is applicable also to cases where our opponents share our language.

the same content). For, if they express different beliefs, then *a* could reject *s*, and we might still not have incompatible beliefs.

By contrast, consider expressivism. Expressivists deny that people must have incompatible beliefs if they are to disagree morally. Thus, given expressivism, a manual that translates *s* with "Capital punishment should be abolished," could be adequate in spite of the fact that *s* and "Capital punishment should be abolished" express different beliefs in our respective languages or idiolects (in so far as they express any beliefs at all).

The same holds for relativist versions of cognitivism. In spite of thinking that moral judgments consist of beliefs, relativists need not think that two persons disagree morally only if they have incompatible beliefs. So, relativism entails that a manual might be adequate even if the sentences of the target idiolect that are translated with our ethical sentences are used to express different beliefs (beliefs with different contents). These conflicting implications regarding the question of which constraints it is plausible to impose on translation manuals will prove crucial in what follows.

### 2.1. EXPLAINING DISAGREEMENTS AWAY

To point out that some moral disagreements are merely apparent is one of the strategies available to a realist who wants to respond to arguments that appeal to moral diversity. Another is to stress that many moral disagreements are not fundamental, because they are rooted in disagreement about *nonmoral* facts. For example, the parties to a discussion about the death penalty may share the view that the death penalty would be justified if it were to deter crime effectively but disagree about whether this is in fact the case.

It might be thought that moral disagreements can be attributed to disagreement over the nonmoral facts only if the parties share basic moral principles.[7] But that is wrong. For example, on one prominent view of moral methodology, we are justified in accepting a basic principle only if it squares with our considered moral judgments "in reflective equilibrium."[8] Thus, consider utilitarianism, and suppose that our considered

---

7 This seems to have been Westermarck's view. See *Ethical Relativity*, Chapter VII, for his views about when disagreements can be explained away.

8 The phrase "reflective equilibrium" is, of course, because of John Rawls. For elaborations of the method of reflective equilibrium, see N. Daniels, "Wide Reflective Equilibrium and Theory Acceptance in Ethics," *Journal of Philosophy* 76 (1979), 256–282 and my *Reflective Equilibrium: An Essay in Moral Epistemology*. Stockholm: Almqvist & Wiksell, 1993.

judgments include the view that the U.S.-led invasion of Iraq in 2003 was illegitimate. According to utilitarianism, roughly, an action is right if and only if it maximizes utility (e.g., happiness). So, whether utilitarianism squares with our judgment about Iraq depends on whether the U.S. invasion *did* maximize utility, which is presumably a nonmoral issue. Hence, a disagreement over a nonmoral issue might affect one's assessment of utilitarianism. This means that settling a nonmoral issue might help to resolve a moral disagreement, even if the parties initially accept different moral principles.[9]

A related strategy is to point out that at least one of the parties to many disputes is subject to a cognitive shortcoming of some sort. For example, it is often held that our concern for our self-interest blurs our minds when we consider moral and political issues. Unsurprisingly, people with high incomes are, in general, more in favor of tax cuts than people with low incomes. From a cynical perspective, this is because people with high incomes have more to gain from the tax cuts, and that their concern for their self-interest leads them to ignore relevant arguments.[10]

Other examples include the influence of prejudice, fear of thinking differently, fallacious reasoning, lack of empathy and lack of imagination. Empathy is required in order to discern which interests are at stake and when someone is harmed. Thus, some animal rights activists have proposed that it should be obligatory for schoolchildren at a certain age to visit a slaughterhouse, so that they may make up their minds on the basis of a more realistic picture of what is going on in the food industry.

As for imagination, a central element in moral reasoning is to formulate general moral principles. Both philosophers and laymen "test" those principles in thought experiments. The idea is that we should ponder a certain possible scenario, apply the theory, and consider whether it yields an intuitively acceptable verdict. This method requires a certain talent for abstract thinking. Moreover, just as is the case in science, imagination is required also as we need to reflect on alternatives to the theory we provisionally start out with. If we adopt a principle simply because we cannot think of an alternative, we are open to rational criticism.

---

9   That the fact that the parties initially accept competing moral principles does not exclude that they can resolve their moral disagreements rationally also is stressed by John Cook. See *Morality and Cultural Differences*, 162–163.

10   See J. T. Lind, "Do the Rich Vote Conservative because They Are Rich?" (http://folk.uio. no/jlind/papers/PartyInc.pdf) for evidence for the correlation between high income and conservative political views.

There is a suggestion that may be more controversial. David Brink argues that one of the considerations that give us reason to be optimistic about the extent to which moral disagreements may be rationally resolvable is the fact that rational agents engage in systematic theoretical reflection. That is, rational agents tend to revise their moral views so as to achieve coherence among them, where this means, roughly, that they are structured through certain evidential and explanatory relations.[11] When engaging in such a process, people may reach agreement, even if they start out with different initial moral beliefs. Accordingly, failure to expose one's moral convictions to this process may count as a shortcoming.

However, several factors contribute to making such reflection potentially difficult. For example, through upbringing, culture and even evolutionary considerations, some people are strongly predisposed to make certain moral judgments. This predisposition may make it difficult to revise them, even in the presence of strong counterarguments.

This is illustrated by a study recently performed by a group of researchers at Princeton University. Consider Philippa Foot's well-known "trolley case."[12] A runaway trolley will kill five people if it is allowed to proceed on its present course. The only way to stop this is to hit a switch that will turn it onto another set of tracks where it will kill one person instead of five. Should you hit the switch? Most people say "yes." At the same time, most people deny that it would be legitimate to stop the trolley by instead pushing a stranger from a footbridge above the tracks (we assume that we cannot stop the trolley by jumping ourselves, since we weigh too little). This may seem surprising. In both cases, we save five persons by sacrificing one, and consistency might seem to require that we judge them similarly.

In trying to explain why people nevertheless judge them differently, one could try to formulate a moral principle according to which there is, after all, a difference. However, the researchers at Princeton choose

---

11  See his *Moral Realism*, Chapter 5. See also Smith, *The Moral Problem*, 155–161. This suggestion is intimately related to coherentism, which, when applied to moral beliefs, is intimately related to the idea of reflective equilibrium. For an illuminating general discussion of coherentism, and of its main competitor (foundationalism), see E. Sosa, "The Raft and the Pyramid: Coherence versus Foundations in the Theory of Knowledge," in P. French, T. Uehling, and H. Wettstein (eds.), *Midwest Studies in Philosophy* 5. Notre Dame: University of Notre Dame Press, 1980, 3–25.

12  "The Problem of Abortion and the Doctrine of the Double Effect," reprinted in *Virtues and Vices*, 19–32.

another approach. They let a number of subjects ponder the different cases, while they at the same time examined their brains, using functional magnetic resonance imaging (fMRI). What they found was that brain areas associated with emotions were more active when the subjects contemplated the footbridge case as compared with when they considered the trolley case. This and similar results led them to a general conclusion, namely, that reflection on "personal" cases – cases that would involve a personal violation – engages people's emotions in a way that "impersonal" cases do not.[13]

If this is true, what is the explanation? According to Peter Singer, the explanation has to do with our evolutionary history. For a long time, human beings lived in small groups, and violence was inflicted only in an up-close way, by "hitting, pushing, strangling, or using a stick or stone as a club."[14] For dealing with these kinds of situations, we have developed immediate, emotionally based responses to cases involving close, personal interactions with others. There has not been an evolutionary pressure to develop similar responses to less personal cases, which explains why the emotions are less involved when we contemplate them.

Peter Singer indicates that he thinks that this account of the intuition about the footbridge case undermines its plausibility, which in turn is relevant to the assessment of his own favorite moral principle (utilitarianism). However, the present point is merely that Greene et al.'s research illustrates that there are mechanisms that may provide an obstacle to the kind of reflection Brink focuses on. This also was corroborated by the fact that the researchers found that the individuals who nevertheless concluded that it was permissible to push the man appeared to do so against a countervailing emotional response, because they exhibited longer reaction times when confronted with the case.

## 2.6. RADICAL MORAL DISAGREEMENT

I call disagreements that can neither be attributed to a cognitive shortcoming of the kind exemplified above nor to nonmoral disagreement "radical moral disagreements." If we combine the radical/nonradical

13  See J. D. Greene, R. B. Sommerville, L. E. Nystrom, J. M. Darley, and J. D. Cohen, "An fMRI Investigation of Emotional Engagement in Moral Judgment," *Science* 293 (2001), 2105–2108.

14  See Singer's "How Reliable are our Moral Intuitions?," *Free Inquiry* 23, (2003), 19–20.

distinction, with the genuine/merely apparent-distinction, we get the following schema:

|                 | Radical | Nonradical |
|-----------------|---------|------------|
| Genuine         | (1)     | (2)        |
| Merely apparent | (3)     | (4)        |

(1) is the crucial square.[15] Suppose that it is empty, and that all (genuine) moral disagreements could be shown to be nonradical. Realists and their opponents alike agree that this would let realists off the hook.[16] Why? As we shall see in the following chapters, the answer depends on which particular version of the argument we have in mind. But a preliminary answer is as follows. The alleged difference between ethics and areas that should be construed realistically is that many disagreements that arise within ethics cannot be rationally resolved. However, if it turns out that all moral disagreements can be attributed to cognitive shortcomings, or to disagreement about nonmoral facts, the contrast disappears.

*Are* there any radical moral disagreements? As one might expect, realists are more optimistic about the possibility of construing existing moral disagreements as nonradical than their critics. Thus, Richard Boyd has said that "careful philosophical examination will reveal [. . .] that agreement on nonmoral issues would eliminate all disagreement about the sorts of issues which arise in ordinary moral practice."[17] Many antirealists, by contrast, think that it is easy to find examples of radical disagreements.[18]

---

15  Of course, both these distinctions can be contested, and perhaps we must allow for gray-zones. For example, Quine's well-known criticism of the analytic/synthetic distinction applies (at least given a cognitivist view) equally well to the genuine/merely apparent-distinction.

16  See, for example, Westermarck, *Ethical Relativity*, 196.

17  "How to Be a Moral Realist," 213. For other optimists, see Brink, *Moral Realism*, 197–209, T. Scanlon, *What We Owe to Each Other*, Cambridge, MA: Belknap Press, 1999, 354–361, and M. Smith, *The Moral Problem*, 187ff and 200ff.

18  See, for example, Harman, "Moral Philosophy and Linguistics," in K. Brinkmann (ed.), *Proceedings of the 20th World Congress of Philosophy, Volume I: Ethics*, Bowling Green, Ohio: Philosophy Documentation Center, 1999, 107–115.

For example, consider the debates between hardcore libertarians such as Robert Nozick, and those who have more egalitarian sympathies, such as John Rawls. Nozick thinks, unlike Rawls, that the structure of a distribution – whether some have a lot whereas others have nothing – is irrelevant to its moral status, and that it is instead determined by how the distribution has come about. Where is the shortcoming?[19]

Another possible candidate is the debate about capital punishment. It has survived many years of discussion, and the opponents are familiar with each other's moves and arguments. Still, the disagreement persists. So, unless one holds a pessimistic view about the cognitive capacities of the parties, we have another example. It is true, of course, that much of the debate concerns deterrence and other empirical considerations, which might seem to indicate that the dispute is not fundamental. But it is not clear that this reflects any agreement about their moral weight. In every debate whose aim is to influence public opinion, many arguments are *ad hominem*. The aim is to show that one's conviction is justified even given the opponent's *own* basic premises. But this need not mean that one shares those premises.

However, one should not underestimate the resources available to a realist.[20] To illustrate this, I shall consider an alleged example of a radical disagreement that has recently been brought to our attention by John Doris and Stephen Stich.[21]

### 2.7. A CULTURE OF HONOR

Doris's and Stich's example concerns an apparent difference between the American South and the American North. It is a well-known fact that certain forms of violence are more frequent in the South. For example, small-town murder rates among friends, lovers, and acquaintances are much higher (more than three times) in the South than in the New England and Midwestern states. The psychologists Richard Nisbett and

---

19 This is one of the disagreements to which the relativist David Wong appeals. See *Moral Relativity*, Chapter 10.

20 For an instructive example of how these resources might be put to work, see Brink, *Moral Realism*, 197–209.

21 The discussion is pursued in their "As a Matter of Fact." However, they stress that the conclusion is tentative and that it might have to be revised. Indeed, this is congenial with their emphasis on the idea of using scientific methods in determining the truth of the empirical claims that are made by philosophers.

Dov Cohen have argued that the difference is best explained by the persistence of a "culture of honor" among contemporary white non-Hispanic Southerners.[22]

In support of their hypothesis, they appeal to the results of certain empirical studies. In one study, letters of application were sent to a number of employers around the United States. The "applicant" purported to be a twenty-seven year-old hardworking Michigan man with a clean record except for one blemish; he had been convicted for manslaughter. He reveals in the letter that he had been in a fight with a man who confronted him in a bar and told onlookers that "he and my fiancée were sleeping together. He laughed at me to my face and asked me to step outside if I was man enough." In the ensuing fight, the man was killed. When assessing the responses they received from the employers, Nisbett and Cohen found that Southerners were much more cooperative than Northerners. One of the Southern employers wrote that "anyone could probably be in the situation you were in. It was just an unfortunate incident that should not be held against you."

These and other of Nisbett's and Cohen's results suggest a disagreement about the appropriate response to insults. People in the South are more tolerant toward a violent response than those in the North. And Doris and Stich suggest that the dispute cannot be explained away in any of the usual ways open for the realists. Thus, they argue that it cannot be attributed to a lack of impartiality or failure to universalize one's judgment, nor to some kind of cognitive impairment or disagreement over the nonmoral facts. For example, the Northerners and Southerners could surely agree that the "applicant" was in fact provoked in the bar.

However, Doris and Stich also stress that there are strategies that they have not considered. For example, realists could appeal to "differences in material circumstance." Let us pursue that suggestion.

One possible difference is this. *Because* of the culture of honor that is in place in the South, a male who does not respond harshly to provocations takes a certain risk. If it becomes known that he cannot or will not retaliate, he faces the risk of being bullied and taken advantage of, and, in particular, of being less highly esteemed by his peers. This in turn may lead to loss of self-esteem, which is a serious loss. Thus, in such a setting, it might be rational for a person to respond violently even to trivial

---

22  See in particular their *Culture of Honor: The Psychology of Violence in the South*. Boulder, CO: Westview Press, 1996.

affronts, since important values are at stake.[23] In a Northern setting, by contrast, these risks are less significant, because the evaluation of a person by others is not so closely connected with the belief that he is able to retaliate in such situations. Because it is usually thought that agents are allowed to assign some weight to their own welfare, this in turn might explain why a violent response is more acceptable in the South than in the North.

According to a related suggestion, what explains the difference is the fact that the South is in general a more violent society. For example, corporal punishment is used more frequently in school discipline in the South than in the North. Moreover, whereas Southern and Northern juries in capital cases recommend the death penalty at equal rates, these sentences are actually carried out more frequently in the South. This reflects the fact that there is a certain familiarity with violence among Southerners, a familiarity that might lead people to underestimate the need for finding a justification in the case of particular acts of violence.

There are further possibilities. Thus, remember Brink's suggestion about the importance of trying to achieve coherence among one's moral convictions and of exposing them to theoretical reflection. It might be argued that neither Northerners nor Southerners have done so to a sufficient extent, and that, if they had, their dispute would have withered. Unless we can rule that out, we cannot be sure that their dispute is radical.

## 2.8. COGNITIVE SHORTCOMINGS

Maybe these suggestions could be ruled out by further research. However, it is easy to think of further explanations. Perhaps it is *too* easy. Both realists and antirealists stress that the truth of the claim that much existing moral disagreement is radical must be determined empirically. But how are we to go about such an investigation? In my view, the way the debate is pursued raises certain methodological worries.

In order to determine that a disagreement is radical we need to specify the factors that are to be counted as cognitive shortcomings. A factor is a candidate in so far as it may plausibly be viewed as diminishing one's

---

23  This is pointed out in D. Cohen, R. Nisbett, B. Bowdle, and N. Schwarz, "Insult, Aggression, and the Southern Culture of Honor: An 'Experimental Ethnography'," *Journal of Personality and Social Psychology* 70 (1996), 945–960.

chances of reaching correct or justified conclusions in moral matters. So, if someone claims that a disagreement can be ignored on the ground that it can be attributed to a certain factor, he should be able to back up this claim with some believable epistemological theory.[24] Notice that the mere fact that a person disagrees with us, or is incorrect about the disputed issue, cannot in itself count as a shortcoming. It would otherwise be easy for a realist to construe every disagreement as nonradical.

Moreover, in order for the claim that a disagreement is radical to be testable, it must hold, for every factor that counts as a shortcoming, that we are able to ascertain whether it is present or not. And in the case of some of the candidates that have been proposed, this is far from clear.

For example, consider again the suggestion that failure to take coherence considerations into account counts as a shortcoming. It might be objected that this suggestion presupposes coherentism, and that coherentism is a controversial doctrine. Brink could respond that it merely presupposes that coherence is *necessary* for justification, not that it is sufficient, which makes it compatible with other theories, such as foundationalism. However, there are those who deny even that it is necessary, at least in the sense of "coherence" assumed by Brink (the sense that requires the acceptance of moral principles).[25]

More important in the present context, the concept of coherence is vague, and, although attempts to explicate it have been made, it is impossible to determine a system's degree of coherence with any accuracy.[26] Accordingly, it is equally difficult to determine when a person has, to a sufficient extent, taken coherence considerations into account. We may always suspect that there are revisions that have not been properly considered, revisions that would make his system even more coherent.

---

24  For example, one could argue that some disagreements involve a shortcoming specifically relevant to the formation of *moral* beliefs. That is, a realist might appeal to a special cognitive faculty by which people may "intuit" moral truths, and argue that one of the parties to a disagreement lacks this faculty, or has failed to exercise it reliably. However, this move is legitimate only if the realist can provide some justification for the claim that we have such a faculty. The problems of this strategy are explored by Crispin Wright in *Truth and Objectivity*, 151–153. See also William Tolhurst's "The Argument from Moral Disagreement," *Ethics* 97 (1987), 610–621.

25  See, for example, Dancy, *Moral Reasons*.

26  For two sophisticated versions of the coherence theory, see Keith Lehrer's *Theory of Knowledge*, London: Routledge, 1990, and Laurence BonJour's *The Structure of Empirical Knowledge*, Cambridge, MA: Harvard University Press, 1985. Yet, none of these versions provides us with a measure of coherence.

Another problem stems from the role of nonmoral beliefs. A moral disagreement is nonradical if at least one of the competing verdicts is based on false beliefs or ignorance about the relevant nonmoral facts. Notice that this condition could be given both in counterfactual and "actualist" terms. Thus, on the one hand, we could say that a moral disagreement is radical only if none of the relevant nonmoral beliefs of the parties is *in fact* false or only if there is *in fact* no relevant nonmoral fact of which they are not informed. On the other hand, we could require merely that the disagreement *would* persist even if they were so informed. In either case, it is difficult, if not impossible, to determine whether the condition is satisfied.

The reason has to do with the fact that the relevant nonmoral issues may be extremely complex. This is clearly true already of questions about the economic effects of tax policies, or the deterring effects of the death penalty. But the problems are even more formidable when we ponder theories according to which the moral status of an action is determined by its consequences for the welfare or happiness of all affected parties. I pointed out above that beliefs about such matters might influence a person's evaluation, not only of an action, but also of principles that assign weight to them (e.g., utilitarianism). If we accordingly require that the parties to a moral disagreement must have true beliefs about the consequences of actions with respect to the total sum of happiness over suffering, to determine that a disagreement is radical requires that *we* are able to determine whether those beliefs *are* true. And given even a quite relaxed view of when a belief is justified, it is doubtful that we have any justified beliefs about such matters, because of problems of measuring happiness, the time perspective, and so on.[27]

A similar problem arises for the counterfactual conception. Given this conception, determining that a disagreement is radical involves determining whether the parties would continue to disagree if they, contrary to fact, were informed about all the relevant nonmoral facts and had pursued the coherence methodology adequately. How can one determine that this holds, given that one neither knows which *are* the relevant facts nor the particulars of the methodology? In view of these difficulties, one may easily be led to think that the disagreement over the extent to which the existing diversity is radical may be just as difficult to resolve as many moral disagreements.

27 For further discussion, see my "Utilitarianism and the Idea of Reflective Equilibrium," *Southern Journal of Philosophy* 29 (1991), 395–406.

We get further support for this suspicion if we turn to intercultural examples. The debates about the death penalty and about abortion are examples of disagreements that occur within Western societies. But some anti-realists rather focus on intercultural ones. Of course, it is not always clear when we face an example of one sort rather than another, in part since it is not clear how to individuate cultures. Still, we may ask whether intercultural disagreements pose an extra problem.

According to one argument to that effect, many of the realist strategies mentioned above are out of place when considering intercultural differences. For example, in the domestic case, there is often background agreement about which nonmoral considerations are relevant in determining a moral issue (say, about the status of the death penalty). This means that disagreements about those issues can be attributed to nonmoral disagreements. In the intercultural case, it may be easier to find examples where there is no such common ground.

However, intercultural disagreements raise certain methodological worries in a way intracultural ones do not. Even if it is difficult to determine whether a moral disagreement is radical in the domestic case, we are seldom in doubt as to whether we face a disagreement in the first place. In the foreign case, by contrast, reports to the effect that people disagree with us may suffer from a certain lack of certainty.

There are different reasons for this. One has to do with problems of identifying and describing the types of actions that the "aliens" are supposed to evaluate morally. There is a worry that we may be too quick to conclude that the classes of actions that we judge to be right or wrong correspond to those being evaluated in the alien culture. For example, we may falsely believe that an expression in the alien language refers to, say, rape, and then conclude that the aliens evaluate rape differently from us on the basis of their use of that expression, whereas it in fact has a quite different extension. Since genuine disputes must concern the evaluation of the very same objects, acts or states of affairs, this would render the dispute merely apparent.[28]

Apart from this problem, moreover, there is a question as to whether the concepts they apply, when we take them to reason morally, can correctly

---

28  Cook calls this "the Projection Error," and suggests that it is has been made especially by relativistically inclined anthropologists. See *Morality and Cultural Differences*, Chapters 9 and 10.

be seen as the counterparts of our concepts of being right, wrong, and so on. Every report to the effect that someone disagrees with us over a moral issue rests on assumptions about when it is reasonable to attribute a moral conviction to other thinkers. Because we get detailed knowledge about the contents of someone's mind only through language, such attributions rely in turn on assumptions about how to interpret their speech; assumptions to the effect that there are expressions in the aliens' idiolect that correspond to our terms "right," "just," and so on. In the domestic case, the question of interpretation seldom arises, as we share the language. In the foreign case, however, we have to rely on a translation manual, formulated by linguists or anthropologists.[29]

Thus, when focusing on the foreign case, we are led to consider the conditions under which such a manual – a manual that translates (or gives the content of) some of the expressions of the target language with (by using) our own evaluative expressions – is adequate or correct. What constraints must it satisfy? This is a crucial question when we ponder the extent to which people disagree morally. For, given the intimate relationship between interpretation and attribution of moral convictions, it entirely determines not only the extent and nature of *actual* moral disagreement that we may encounter, but also the range of *possible* disagreement.

I call views that state the conditions that an adequate translation manual must satisfy (i.e., views that state the conditions under which moral judgments could correctly be attributed to another thinker) "attributional principles." To illustrate how our attributional principles determine the extent and nature of the moral disagreement that we may encounter, I shall briefly consider an example.

A number of attempts have been made to use Donald Davidson's views on meaning and interpretation to show that the extent of moral disagreement is exaggerated.[30] Davidson is known for the thesis that there is, necessarily, considerable overlap between the systems of belief of different thinkers.[31] The idea is that this thesis applies also to moral convictions.

---

29  Some theorists stress that the distinction is imaginary, and that the problem of interpretation arises also "at home."

30  See, for example, D. Cooper, "Moral Relativism," *Midwest Studies in Philosophy* 3 (1978), 97–108; S. Hurley, "Objectivity and Disagreement," in Honderich, *Morality and Objectivity*, 54–97; and J. Stout, *Ethics After Babel*. Boston: Beacon Press, 1988, Chapter 1.

31  See, for example, his *Subjective, Intersubjective, Objective*. Oxford: Oxford University Press, 2001, essays 10 and 11.

Davidson's argument for his convergence thesis relies on the so-called principle of charity.[32] Davidson's project is to illuminate the concept of meaning. This in turn prompts him to adopt the perspective of an interpreter, and to focus on the following question: how could someone achieve knowledge of the meanings of another speaker's sentences? Davidson thinks that such knowledge can be captured by a "theory of interpretation" for the speaker; that is, a finitely axiomatized theory that entails for each sentence $s$ of the target idiolect a "T-sentence" which is a theorem of the form

$s$ is true in the speaker's idiolect if and only if $p$.

where "$s$" is replaced by a description of $s$, and $p$ is replaced by a sentence of the metalanguage (the interpreter's language) which is true if and only if $s$ is.[33] The question is when such a theory is justified. This is where the principle of charity enters.

More specifically, the principle of charity comprises a set of constraints on theories of interpretation. Among other things, it entails that a theory is correct only if it assigns truth conditions such that the sentences the speaker holds to be true, in general, *are* true, by our, the interpreters' lights. For example, if we notice that the speaker is selectively caused to hold a sentence true by the presence of rain, we should try for a theory that entails that the sentence is true if and only if it is raining.[34]

A central theme in Davidson's philosophy is that the project of determining the meanings of a speaker's sentences, and the project of uncovering what he believes, goes hand in hand. This is evident from the fact that, given information about which sentences the speaker accepts, a theory of interpretation also yields a theory about what he believes. So, for example, if the speaker accepts a sentence that is true if and only if it rains, we may conclude that he believes that it is raining.[35] A consequence is

32 The principle of charity also has been defended by David Lewis and W. V. O. Quine. See Lewis, "Radical Interpretation," in his *Philosophical Papers* (vol. 1), Oxford: Oxford University Press, 1983, 108–121, 112; and W. V. O. Quine, *Word and Object*. Cambridge, MA: MIT Press, 1960, 59 and 69.

33 See, for example, *Inquiries into Truth and Interpretation*, essays 9–11, and "The Structure and Content of Truth," *Journal of Philosophy* 87 (1990), 279–328.

34 See *Inquiries into Truth and Interpretation*, essays 9–11. Notice, however, that particular assignments are not to be tested in isolation, not even at the observational level. Rather, they are tested "holistically." Whether an assignment is correct depends on whether it is entailed by a theory that as a whole explains the relevant evidence better than alternative ones.

35 Davidson writes that "sentence held true plus interpretation [i.e., an assigment of truth conditions] equals belief" ("Toward a Unified Theory of Meaning and Action," 6). See also *Expressing Evaluations*, The Lindley Lecture, published as monograph. Lawrence: University

that the principle of charity can be stated directly in terms of belief attribution. Although it does not exclude the attribution of error altogether, it entails that we interpret a person correctly only if we represent him as agreeing with us about most matters (i.e., as, by and large, having beliefs that are consistent and true, by our lights). The underlying idea is vividly expressed as follows:

[H]ow clear are we that the ancients – some ancients – believed that the earth was flat? *This* earth? Well, this earth of ours is part of the solar system, a system partly identified by the fact that it is a gaggle of large, cool, solid bodies circling around a very large, hot star. If someone believes *none* of this about the earth, is it certain that it is the earth that he is thinking about? An answer is not called for. The point is made if this kind of consideration of related beliefs can shake one's confidence that the ancients believed the earth was flat.[36]

On the basis of the principle of charity, Davidson concludes that extensive disagreement between the systems of belief of different thinkers may be excluded. And in some recent papers, he emphasizes that the principle is to be applied not only to "our so-called factual judgments" but also to evaluative ones. Thus, in "Objectivity and Practical Reason", he writes that "we should expect enlightened values [. . .] to converge: we should expect people who are enlightened and who fully understand one another's words to agree on many basic values", and a little later:

These considerations do not, of course, show that there can be no real differences in norms among those who understand each other. There can be, as long as the differences can be seen to be real because placed within a common framework. The common framework is the area of overlap, of norms one person correctly interprets another as sharing. [. . .] Good interpretation makes for convergence then, and on values in particular.[37]

Others have reached similar conclusions. In particular, Davidson's views have been taken to exclude *radical* moral disagreement.[38] As I just wrote, the principle of charity does not exclude the attribution of errors altogether. However, Davidson has stressed that an error is to be attributed

of Kansas, 1984, 17, "On Quine's Philosophy," *Theoria* 60 (1994), 184–192, 190, and "The Myth of the Subjective," reprinted in *Subjective, Intersubjective, Objective*, 39–53, 165.

36  *Inquiries into Truth and Interpretation*, 168.

37  Pages 24ff. See also "The Objectivity of Values," in C. Gutierrez (ed.), *El Trabajo Filosofico de Hoy en el Continente*. Bogota: Editorial ABC, 1995, 59–69, and Lars Bergström's and Dagfinn Føllesdal's "Interview with Donald Davidson," *Theoria*, 60 (1994), 207–225.

38  See, for example, Cooper, "Moral Relativism," Hurley, "Objectivity and Disagreement," and J. Stout, *Ethics After Babel*, Chapter 1.

only if there is some believable explanation of *why* the agent is mistaken, in terms of some cognitive shortcoming that he is subject to.[39] Because none of the parties to a radical disagreement is subject to such a shortcoming, and because at least one of the parties to a genuine disagreement is in error, we can, it is held, rule out the existence of genuine and radical moral disagreements.[40]

## 2.10. THE STATUS OF ATTRIBUTIONAL PRINCIPLES

This reasoning illustrates the relevance of one's attributional principles in the present context. It can obviously be contested. Davidson's views are controversial, and, even if we assume that they are correct for nonmoral contexts,[41] it is doubtful if they can be applied to evaluative expressions.

In fact, a central claim in the present essay is that they cannot. In particular, I shall argue that the principle of charity is not relevant to the attribution of moral convictions in the way presupposed by Davidson. Suppose that we are convinced that the death penalty is morally wrong. Davidson suggests that we are entitled to attribute a conflicting view to another agent only if we may assume that he agrees with us about many other moral issues, and in particular about which (nonmoral) considerations are relevant in determining the moral status of the death penalty. Thus, he stresses that a moral disagreement is "genuine only when there are shared criteria in the light of which there is an answer to the question who is right."[42] By contrast, according to the view that I favor, when we attribute moral convictions to others, we may allow for considerable latitude. That is, we may attribute a specific moral conviction to a person, whether or not we share it, even in the absence of shared criteria and

---

39 See "Objectivity and Practical Reason," 25, and *Inquiries*, 196. For a similar view, see Lewis, "Radical Interpretation," 112.
40 I shall return to this reasoning in Chapter 4. Geoffrey Sayre-McCord has objected to attempts to support claims about convergence in ethics with reference to the principle of charity by pointing out that it merely requires our finding *most* of the speaker's beliefs as true, and that this is consistent with finding him mostly wrong in certain restricted areas (such as ethics). ("Being a Realist about Relativism (in Ethics)," *Philosophical Studies* 61 (1991), 155–176, (note 6). Sayre-McCord thus interprets the claim that most of an agent's beliefs must be true as analogous to the claim that most Canadians are English-speaking when we take it to be compatible with the fact that French is more common in Quebec. However, the principle of charity clearly entails that it holds for *every* predicate that figures in the speaker's beliefs that most of the beliefs that involve that predicate are true, as the above example with the earth indicates.
41 I discuss the plausibility of this assumption in Chapter 5.
42 "Objectivity and Practical Reason," 25.

extensive overlap in basic values and norms, and even if it is based on quite different considerations than those we take to be relevant. Moreover, a translation manual that represents someone as disagreeing with us over a moral issue may be correct even if his judgment cannot be explained in terms of some cognitive shortcoming of deficiency. This is the upshot of "the latitude idea" that was mentioned in the Preface and again in Chapter 1.

What might give us a reason to prefer the latitude idea to the Davidsonian view? Given their different implications for the question of the nature and extent of the moral disagreement that we may encounter, this is a crucial question. The really important question is, of course, whether it is possible to provide an *independent* justification. For, if it turns out that the assumption that there is radical moral disagreement presupposes attributional principles whose justification in turn relies on an antirealist view on moral discourse, we cannot, obviously, appeal to this assumption in order to refute realism.

Still, in Chapter 6, I shall argue that we *can* provide independent support for attributional principles. In particular, I shall argue that there is such support for the latitude idea, which in turn is a crucial premise in my argument against moral realism. The argument is related to the suggestion that assumptions about the nature of moral convictions should be assessed in the context of a wider psychological theory, whose aim is to explain behavior in general and not just the kind of evidence to which meta-ethical theories are usually supposed to be responsive.

More specifically, given this suggestion, the plausibility of an assumption about the nature moral judgments depends on whether the states it picks out as moral judgments are assigned a distinct explanatory role by such a theory. If so, and if the theory is vindicated by the evidence (*all* the evidence), so is this assumption. If not, it should be rejected. As for the latitude idea, it is not in itself sufficient for picking out a determinate set of states. The question is instead whether the fact that a set of states are different in the sense allowed for by the latitude idea excludes that they have a distinct explanatory role in the required sense. I shall argue that it does not. The point of departure of my argument is that the role assigned to moral convictions by an adequate theory of human behavior is to help explain why people manage to coordinate their actions in a mutually beneficial way in response to certain types of collective action problems.[43]

---

43  I am not the first to suggest that reflections on when to attribute moral judgements might shed light over their nature. See, for example, Boyd, "How To Be a Moral Realist," 210f,

So, are there any radical moral disagreements? The important result of the discussions in this chapter is that answering this question requires addressing a number of complex philosophical questions, in epistemology and philosophy of language. This theory-dependence renders the project of determining the extent to which the existing moral diversity is radical problematic. Indeed, there is even an issue as to whether the existence of radical moral disagreement can be established independently of taking a stand in the debate about realism that we are trying to adjudicate. The nature of moral disagreement depends on which attributional principles are correct, and, as we saw in 2.3, different meta-ethical positions are associated with different sets of such principles. So intimately, in fact, that any argument that appeals to moral disagreement must be closely scrutinized with respect to potential question-beggingness.

Of course, it might be questioned whether it holds for each of the alleged shortcomings surveyed above that its presence really does let realists off the hook. Maybe a disagreement can undermine realism even if it is not radical in the rather special sense that has been explored in this chapter. That possibility cannot be ruled out before we get a better grasp of *why* radical moral disagreements are supposed to show realism to be false.

Dworkin, "Objectivity and Truth: You'd Better Believe It," 116, Gibbard, *Wise Choices*, 101, Hare, *The Language of Morals*, 148ff, R. Miller, *Moral Differences*. Princeton, NJ: Princeton University Press, 1992, 95–101, and Smart, *Ethics, Persuasion, and Truth*, 29–34. Notice that these writers appeal to such considerations in defense of quite different theses.

# 3

# *Explaining and Predicting Disagreement*

## 3.1. INTRODUCTION

The well-known moral realist Nicholas Sturgeon once wrote that any critical response to a philosophical position can be classified as either an "Oh yeah?" or a "So what?"[1] In the case of the claim that much moral diversity is radical, and therefore less tractable than disagreements in other areas, realists usually pursue the "Oh yeah?"–line. In this chapter, however, I shall start to explore the "So what?"–response. *Why* is the diversity supposed to show that there are no objective moral facts?

According to one idea, the reason is that the latter claim provides the *best explanation* of the diversity. For example, in David Brink's view, the central premise is the thesis that "moral disputes are so pervasive and so intractable that the best explanation of this kind of disagreement is that there are no moral facts."[2]

Brink conceives of this as an *a posteriori* argument; as an argument that relies on premises whose evaluation requires empirical research.[3] There are versions that are construed differently, versions that appeal to the mere

---

1 He says that he has it "on good authority" (i.e., his graduate students). See "What Difference Does it Make Whether Moral Realism is True?," *Southern Journal of Philosophy* 24 (suppl.) (1986), 115–141, 115.

2 *Moral Realism*, 197.

3 Many agree with Brink in construing the argument in this way. See, for example, Doris and Stich, "As a Matter of Fact." See also Cook's *Morality and Cultural Differences*. Cook discusses extensively whether the empirical evidence regarding existing moral diversity supports moral relativism. It should be noted, however, that Cook conceives of relativism as the claim that correct moral principles involve a "relativizing clause" and that a person's conduct can rightly be judged according to them only if he is covered by that clause (see pp. 14ff). This is a normative claim rather than a meta-ethical one, which means that much of the discussion in Cook's book is not directly relevant to my concerns.

43

*possibility* of radical disagreement. However, this chapter is devoted to versions that appeal to claims about the *existing* diversity. I shall argue that none of these versions strengthens anti-realism to any significant extent.

## 3.2. THE ARGUMENT FROM RELATIVITY

Many realists concede that, if a significant number of the existing moral disagreements were radical, realism would be in trouble, at least if we assume that this would mean that they cannot be rationally resolved. For example, Brink holds that "[i]t is incumbent on the moral realist [. . .] to claim that *most* moral disputes are resolvable at least in principle."[4] But this generous concession is possibly based on his optimism about the possibility of establishing that claim.

Yet, maybe Brink's concession is premature. Consider the suggestion that it is the absence of objective moral facts that explains moral disagreement. At first, this suggestion might strike one as a bit odd. Could the *absence* of certain facts have effects of that sort? Many who are inclined to reject realism rather stress that the best explanation of why people disagree morally is that they belong to different social groups, or that they have different upbringings, or some similar fact. Such explanations do not seem to presuppose the claim that there are no moral facts, nor any other philosophical doctrine.

But perhaps the appeal to explanation is more indirect. In this section, I shall consider the argument that provides the point of departure of Brink's discussion, namely J. L. Mackie's well-known "argument from relativity." This is one of the arguments to which Mackie appeals in support of his "error theory"; that is, the claim that, although moral claims purport to describe facts, there are no facts in virtue of which they can be true.

Mackie begins his discussion as follows:

The argument from relativity has as its premiss the well-known variation in moral codes from one society to another and from one period to another, and also the differences in moral beliefs between different groups and classes within a complex community.[5]

---

4 *Moral Realism*, 200. What does "resolvable" mean here? It may seem natural to assume that a dispute is resolvable if and only if there is a fact of the matter as to who is correct, in which case Brink's claim about what realism entails is obviously true. However, it is not this notion that Brink has in mind. Rather, in Brink's view, whether a dispute is resolvable depends on whether the parties could come to agree as a result of rational argumentation or the implementation of some kind of rational method.

5 *Ethics*, 36.

Mackie emphasizes that there is no direct step from the diversity to his skepticism about objective values. Taken by itself, the variation of moral codes is just a fact of anthropology, and he stresses that the disputes that occur in the sciences do not prompt an antirealist conclusion.

However, there is, he thinks, a crucial difference between scientific disagreements and those that occur in ethics. In science, the disagreement "results from speculative inferences or explanatory hypotheses based on inadequate evidence." According to Mackie, this is not a plausible diagnosis of the disagreements that arise in ethics. Therefore, moral disagreement supports moral skepticism:

[T]he argument from relativity has some force simply because the actual variations in the moral codes are more readily explained by the hypothesis that they reflect ways of life than by the hypothesis that they express perceptions, most of them seriously inadequate and badly distorted, of objective values.[6]

In other words, according to Mackie, there are two competing hypotheses. The first hypothesis states that our moral codes reflect our "way of life." For example, "people approve of monogamy because they participate in a monogamous life" rather than the other way round.[7] Mackie acknowledges that there are persons "who have turned against the established rules and practices of their own communities." But that can, according to Mackie, be

understood as the extension, in ways which, though new and unconventional, seemed to them to be required for consistency, of rules to which they already adhered as arising out of an existing way of life.[8]

According to the second hypothesis, by contrast, our moral judgments are better seen as responses to, or perceptions of, objectively existing moral facts. Why does the realist have to construe them as "seriously inadequate and badly distorted"? The reason is that, given a realist view, if people have conflicting judgments, some of them must be false. Thus, in order to hold on to the idea that these judgments are perceptions of moral facts, a realist has to invoke the idea of a distorted perception.

Mackie dismisses the second hypothesis without much ado. He seems to think that the idea of blaming the disagreement on speculative inferences or something similar is in many cases just too far-fetched to be taken

6  *Ethics*, 37.
7  *Ethics*, 36.
8  *Ethics*, 36f.

seriously. Let us for a moment concede this view, and instead focus on another question. The first hypothesis is a claim about the causal background of our moral judgments. Let us call it "the genetical claim." The question is: why does the truth of the genetical claim undermine realism? This may not be obvious. After all, realism is a thesis about the status of moral judgments, not about their causal background.

However, one way to bring out its relevance is as follows. It is sometimes held that we have reason to accept a (philosophical) thesis if it is entailed by the best explanation of some state of affairs whose existence can be established independently of what we think about the thesis in question. Now, relative to moral realism, the fact that we have formed a certain moral judgment *is* such a state of affairs. For we may determine that someone *thinks*, say, that it is wrong to torture cats prior to determining both whether it is wrong and whether there are any moral truths. So, if the best explanation of why someone holds a moral judgment entails that the judgment is true, we have evidence not only for that particular judgment, but also for the general (realist) claim that there are moral truths. This would be a powerful argument for realism.

However, the genetical claim deprives the realist of this argument. For if it is true, then we can explain why people have formed their moral judgments by appealing to their "ways of life," and such explanations do not invoke any moral facts.[9] Thus, given the genetical claim, one way of justifying moral realism is blocked.

As the observant reader notices, this reasoning is congenial with a famous argument of Gilbert Harman's. Harman's point of departure is the idea that we have no reason to believe in the existence of a class of entities unless those entities are assumed by the best explanation of something observable. However, although the fact that we have formed a given moral judgment *is* something observable, when we explain such facts, we never need to assume that the judgment in question is true. For example, suppose that a person sees some children who pour gasoline on a cat and ignite it, and forms the judgment that what is happening is wrong. According to Harman, we may explain this fact satisfactorily by appealing to the person's upbringing and moral sensibility, and do not have to assume anything about the moral status of the children's act.[10]

---

9 We must assume here that the best explanation of "our way of life" does not in turn presuppose any moral claims.

10 Again, notice that what is to be explained is the fact that we *think* that the children's behavior is wrong, not that it *is* wrong.

Harman concludes that we have no reason to believe in the existence of moral facts.[11]

What does this have to do with disagreement? At best, the relevance is very indirect. For example, Harman does not rely on considerations about disagreement. Instead, he appeals to a kind of parsimony (do not posit an entity unless you have to!), and to the absence of a believable account of *how* the truth of a moral judgment is supposed to have an impact on our thinking.[12]

Moreover, although Mackie does appeal to disagreement, the route to the antirealist conclusion is long and winding. Mackie believes that the best explanation of the "actual variations in the moral codes" is provided by the genetical claim; that is, the claim that they "reflect our way of life," which means that the genetical claim obtains support from the variation. And the genetical claim suggests in turn that the best explanation of why we form moral judgments never assumes that such judgments are true. This claim, finally, undermines one possible way of justifying moral realism.

There are accordingly plenty of options for someone who wants to reject the argument. For example, one may point out that just because *one* way of justifying realism is blocked this does not exclude that there may be other ways. Moreover, it is not at all obvious that the actual variation *does* provide support for the genetical claim. To determine this requires a more detailed account of the genetical claim. Before it has been clarified we simply don't know under what conditions it predicts variation.

For example, notice that it predicts variation only to the extent that people's ways of life differ. So, the "actual variation of moral codes" supports the genetical claim only if people's ways of life differ in accordance with their moral codes. And if it is found that people disagree even if they have the same way of life, which may hold for many intracultural disagreements, we seem to have refuted the genetical claim. For example, some Americans talk of an "American way of life." It might accordingly be argued that the fact that Americans still disagree over many moral issues squares badly with the genetical claim. Mackie could respond by insisting that these Americans do not share the same way of life in the *relevant*

11  See *The Nature of Morality*. New York: Oxford University Press, 1977, Chapter 1. Notice, however, that the criticism is limited to nonrelativist and nonreductionist versions of realism. Given a relativist or reductionist construal of moral facts, he neither denies that they exist nor that they can figure in the best explanations of our moral judgments.

12  See "Moral Explanations of Natural Facts – Can Moral Claims Be Tested Against Moral Reality?," *Southern Journal of Philosophy* 24 (suppl.) (1986), 57–68, 62.

sense. But then we need a clear conception of what the relevant sense *is*. Before we have such a conception, the theory sketched by Mackie is not testable.

Of course, there have been other attempts to account for our moral judgments without invoking moral facts. Thus, consider Marvin Harris's much discussed explanation of female infanticide, for example among the Yanomamö (the Amazon people mentioned in the Preface).[13] According to Harris, the explanation of this practice has ultimately to do with access to protein. The Yanomamö live in an environment where protein is scarce. So there is a need to regulate the population, which partly accounts for the killings of female infants. As an effect of these killings there is a shortage of women, which prompts Yanomamö men to raid each other's villages. This leads to a selective advantage to warlike societies and explains the admiration of and preference for fierce males, which in turn sustains the practice of female infanticide.

Harris's account has been criticized on several grounds. For example, Napoleon Chagnon and Raymond Hames have objected that it squares badly with the evidence, because the Yanomamö in fact do not suffer from protein scarcity, at least not to the extent that Harris's model assumes.[14] Moreover, Chagnon points out that there is in fact little evidence for population regulation among the Yanomamö, who at the time of his main study had a rather high rate of population growth (c. 3 percent per annum). In view of these objections, I think a sober assessment of Harris's proposal (and one with which Harris would probably agree) is that it at best provides a *fragment* of an antirealist account of our moral judgments. It identifies one of the factors that may be important in the development of the morality of a given culture. However, given, for example, the existence of moral differences within a culture, it clearly lacks resourses to explain the moral judgments of individuals. Therefore, it is difficult to test it by seeing how much disagreement (or agreement) it predicts.

Are there any other theories? Allan Gibbard suggests in his seminal book *Wise Choices, Apt Feelings* that our propensity for moral thinking could be explained by evolutionary considerations. Roughly, it has evolved as it helps us resolve certain collective action problems. This may

13  See M. Harris, *Cannibals and Kings*, New York: Random House, 1977, and "Animal Capture and Yanamamo Warfare: Retrospect and New Evidence," *Journal of Anthropological Research* 40 (1984), 183–201. The Yanomamö and their ways were mentioned in the Preface. For an account of the Yanomamö culture, see Chagnon, *Yanomamö*.
14  N. A. Chagnon and R. Hames, "Protein Deficiency and Tribal Warfare in Amazonia: New Data," *Science* 203 (1979), 910–913.

or may not be true. However, again, even if true, Gibbard's account does not say anything about why particular individuals form *specific* judgments. And this is what we need in order to test it by considering how much moral disagreement it predicts. The truth is, in my view, that we lack a theory of the formation of moral codes and judgments that allows for such testing. So, if the inference from moral disagreement to antirealism presupposes the existence of such a theory, we may, at the present stage, safely resist it.

### 3.3. BY WHAT MECHANISM?

However, maybe the advocate of the argument does not really have to produce such a theory. The underlying thought of the above reasoning is that facts about moral disagreement indicate that moral truths never figure in the best explanation of our moral judgments. But such facts could provide support for that conclusion in two different ways. Either by supporting theories that don't invoke any moral facts (such as Mackie's "way of life"–theory), or by undermining explanations that *do*.

Notice that it is really the latter of these strategies that Harman pursues. To be sure, Harman talks a little about the role of upbringing and moral sensibilities.[15] But he does not rely on those speculations. Instead, he challenges the realist to tell us *how* moral facts are supposed to affect our thinking. In the absence of a believable account of the relevant mechanism, he suggests, we should be skeptical toward accounts of our moral judgments that invoke moral facts.

For example, Harman considers a case where Jane sees that Albert hits a cat with a stick:

What's needed is some account of *how* the actual wrongness of Albert's action could help to explain Jane's disapproval of it. And we have to be able to believe in this account. We cannot just make something up, saying, for example, that the wrongness of the act affects the quality of the light reflected into Jane's eyes, causing her to react negatively. That would be an example of wrongness manifesting itself in the world in a way that could serve as evidence for and against certain moral claims, but it is not something we can believe in.[16]

Although Harman himself does not appeal to considerations about moral disagreement in this context, it may be argued that they have some

---

15   See *The Nature of Morality*, 4.
16   "Moral Explanations of Natural Facts," 62.

49

relevance. Suppose that *a* and *b* disagree about Albert's behavior – *a* thinks that it is appropriate, whereas *b* thinks that it is wrong. This means that, from a realist point of view, *a* and *b* have incompatible beliefs. Hence, it cannot hold for *each* of the verdicts that it is best explained by assuming that it is true.

This need not be a problem in itself, of course. No one has demanded that *all* moral judgments must be explained by their truth in order for realism to be justified. However, it does pose a challenge to the realist. For it means that he must provide an account that is capable of explaining the emergence of *false* judgments. That is, he must explain errors in a way compatible with thinking that *other* judgments are best explained by their truth. In the present case, he has to point to some *difference* between the ways *a*'s and *b*'s verdicts were formed that justifies two explanatory strategies.

In comparison, consider color judgments. It might be argued that, in the case of colors, there *is* a believable account of the relevant mechanism. The fact that some object is, say, red entails that its surface has a certain structure. This structure is responsible for the fact that the surface, when illuminated with white light, reflects photons at certain wavelengths while absorbing others. When we are rightly placed, the light reflected by the object hits the retinas of our eyes, and causes, through the optical nerve, certain cerebral processes in the visual cortex and other parts of our brains. Eventually, we are led to believe that the object is red. This account justifies us in thinking that the fact that we believe that an object is red is, in some cases, best explained by the assumption that the object *is* red, or so it might be held.

Of course, there are occasional disagreements also about an object's color, which means that realists about color face the same challenge as realists about values. But such disagreements can always, it is held, be attributed to some feature that indicates that the relevant mechanism has malfunctioned, or is somehow out of play. For example, the perceptual conditions might have been unfavorable, or the eyes of one of the parties might not function properly. Such disagreements do not undermine the idea that there is a mechanism of the relevant kind, as they do not undermine the claim that, under *appropriate* conditions, if a person were confronted with an item, he would recognize its true color.

In the moral case, it is also sometimes reasonable to attribute disagreement to factors that are analogous to unfavorable perceptual conditions. However, in so far as there are disagreements that cannot be treated in this way – in so far as the disagreements are radical – they undermine the idea that there is a mechanism corresponding to that involved in the case of colors. This is why, according to the present reasoning, it is crucial for a realist to show that all existing disagreements in ethics are non-radical.

Are there really no radical disagreements in the case of colors? It might be thought that this is a contingent, empirical issue. However, it also might be argued that it depends on certain considerations having to do with the interpretation and meaning of color terms.

Reconsider the Davidsonian view about belief attribution mentioned at the end of Section 2.9. According to this view, if someone disagrees with us about the application of a term *t* we are entitled to conclude that *t* has the same reference in our respective idiolects only if we have reason to think that his (alleged) error is explicable; that is, as resulting from a cognitive shortcoming of some sort. If we apply this view to color terms, we are able to rule out the existence of (genuine) radical disagreements about colors *a priori*. If someone applies "red" to a blue object, and we cannot attribute his verdict to unfavorable conditions or anything of that sort, we should conclude that his "red" means something different from ours, rather than that he disagrees with us about the color of the object.

However, in order for this reasoning to provide the sought-for contrast between ethics and other areas (areas that we want to be realists about), we have to deny that it is available in ethics. I am in sympathy with that view. This is what the latitude idea is all about. However, notice that, if this is the contrast, it does not hinge in any straightforward way on empirical considerations, which undermines the *a posteriori* status of the argument.

Moreover, to point out that a realist has to develop an account of how moral facts are supposed to have an impact on our thinking that allows us to explain the emergence of error amounts to little more than a rehearsal of Harman's demand. Furthermore, it interprets this demand rather strongly. It requires that a realist must show that there is a set of conditions such that, if anyone were to be confronted with a moral fact under those conditions, he would recognize that it obtains. Maybe one could argue that a judgment could be best explained by its truth in spite of the fact that we lack reason to believe that there are any such conditions. With all these questions left unanswered, any conclusion about the role of moral disagreement in this particular context is seriously premature.

Let us try another tack. I said above that it sounds odd to say that the absence of moral facts explains why people disagree morally. However, maybe the oddness disappears if we rephrase the explanandum. It might be less odd to say that the absence of moral facts explains why there is *more* disagreement in ethics than in other areas, or why it is less easy to *resolve* those disagreements.

Similarly, it does not seem so odd to say that the fact that people manage to *agree* in an area depends on the existence of truths in that area. Indeed, this is a claim many are inclined to accept. Thus, according to one prominent argument for scientific realism, even if there is disagreement also in science, over time, scientists tend to resolve their differences. This convergence is best explained, it is held, by assuming that there are truths for scientists to discover.[17]

Of course, even if agreement in an area *may* provide a reason to accept realism about that area, it does not automatically lead to such a conclusion. The agreement could be because of irrational factors, such as a lack of courage to dissent. The fact that people have a tendency to work their way to a consensus, even in cases where there is no evidence one way or the other, is well documented. For example, consider the classic experiments of M. A. Sherif. Sherif found that a number of individuals initially perceived very different movements when a spot of light was projected in a dark room in such a way that it appeared to move. However, when they had to describe the movements to the rest of the group, their judgments tended to converge.[18] Similarly, the psychologist S. E. Asch has found that a minority of subjects would disbelieve their judgments of length – judgments they otherwise made accurately – when a majority of planted subjects had agreed on something different. Surely, when agreement in an area is a result of the mechanisms that seem involved in these experiments, it provides little support for realism.[19]

Indeed, that this would be the case for convergence in ethics, if any should occur, is suggested by Bernard Williams:

The basic idea behind the distinction between the scientific and the ethical, expressed in terms of convergence, is very simple. In a scientific inquiry there

---

17   For this line of reasoning, see, for example, Newton-Smith, W., *The Rationality of Science*, London: Routledge, 1981.

18   See his *The Psychology of Social Norms*, New York: Harper & Row, 1936.

19   *Social Psychology*, New York: Prentice Hall, 1952.

should be convergence on an answer, where the best explanation of the convergence involves the idea that the answer represents how things are; in the area of the ethical [. . .] there is no such coherent hope. The distinction does not turn on any difference in whether convergence will actually occur, and it is important that this is not what the answer is about. It might well turn out that there is convergence in ethical outlook, at least among human beings. The point of the contrast is that, even if this happens, it will not be correct to think it has come about because convergence has been guided by how things actually are, whereas convergence in the sciences might be explained that way if it does happen.[20]

How can he be sure? Presumably, whether the best explanation of possible future convergence in ethics would assume the existence of moral facts depends on the circumstances. It depends in part on whether there is reason to believe that it would be due to mechanisms such as those that were operating in the cases studied by Sherif and Asch. Williams might respond that explanations that invoke moral facts can be ruled out *a priori* since there are no moral facts. But then the above remarks provide a *characterization* of his antirealism rather than an argument for it.

If we instead are looking for an argument, we might reason as follows. The existence of convergence in ethics would, possibly, provide support for moral realism. So the absence of convergence deprives realists of that argument. Thus, disagreement (indirectly) supports antirealism.

However, this means that, for the third time, we have ended up with an indirect argument. Moreover, it is an indirect argument whose weight can be contested. The fact that there is disagreement on many moral issues must, in the present context, be weighed against the fact that there is also much agreement; a consideration that might supply the realists with material for the sought-for pro-argument. For example, it is often noted that, in many societies, some issues that used to be controversial (such as slavery and female voting) are so no longer.[21] Maybe there is a preemptive explanation of this agreement of the kind Williams imagines. For example, maybe the best explanation invokes the mechanisms researched by Asch and Sherif. But that remains to be shown.

---

20  *Ethics and the Limits of Philosophy*, London: Fontana, 1985, 136.
21  See, for example, Brink, *Moral Realism*, 208. Moreover, Michael Smith has suggested that some agreement has become so stable so as to be reflected in language. Thus, consider "thick" terms, such as "courageous." The fact that such words can be used to convey information about the nonmoral properties of agents manifests the fact that there is agreement about how to evaluate these properties or people who have them. See *The Moral Problem*, 188.

What are the prospects for a more direct argument? The idea that agreement in an area may be best explained by assuming that what one agrees on is true suggests that the existence of truths may, in certain cases, lead us to expect agreement. After all, explanation and prediction are sides of the same coin. This in turn may seem to suggest that there would have been (more) agreement in ethics, if there *had* been moral facts. And, given that claim, it may seem that the disagreement is, after all, explained by the assumption that there are no moral facts.[22]

Why believe that there would have been (more) convergence in ethics, if there had been moral facts? That thesis is even difficult to comprehend. However, according to one suggestion, we should accept it since there is reason to believe that it holds *generally* that if there are facts in an area, then people will, sooner or later, recognize these facts. For example, David Wiggins suggests that "[i]f X is true, then X will under favourable circumstances command convergence," regardless, it seems, of what we should replace X with.[23] The idea is that the existence of truths in a given area somehow *constrains* the beliefs we are disposed to form in that area. Maybe facts are supposed to function as teachers of schoolchildren. When the teacher is around, we can expect the children to behave better (i.e., more homogenously) than when he or she is away.

However, in the case of the teacher, we know something about the underlying mechanisms. Do we have such an account in the case of facts? Presumably, the account has to be epistemological. I said above that it does not sound so odd to say that the absence of correct answers to a set of issues may help to explain why people cannot resolve their disagreements about those issues. For example, I have been told that believers in Atlantis disagree about its location. Some say that it was located close to the island Santorini in the Aegean Sea, whereas others think that it was located in the Atlantic. Why haven't they been able to settle their dispute? Part of the explanation might be that there is no evidence that allows us to decide the matter.[24] But the best explanation of that in turn might be that

---

22  Of course, because the existence of facts is never sufficient for convergence, the explanation of the lack of agreement can also invoke other assumptions.

23  *Needs, Values, Truth,* 147.

24  We presuppose here that the thinkers are responsive to evidence in forming their beliefs. This is what makes it plausible to hold that if there *had* been such evidence, then they would have resolved their dispute. Maybe this assumption is too optimistic.

there never *was* an Atlantis. For if it *had* existed, it would have left some traces.[25]

The underlying thought is in other words that if there are truths in an area, people will obtain *knowledge* of them, at least in the long run, and if they are not subject to any distorting factor. This explains Wiggins's emphasis on "favorable circumstances," and why the advocates of the argument from disagreement focus on radical disagreement.[26] The (alleged) fact that people disagree radically is supposed to show that there are no moral facts. For if there had been any moral facts, they would have been detectable, at least for people who are not subject to cognitive shortcomings such as bias, self-interest, and so on. Hence, they would not have disagreed.

A problem with this argument is that the idea that facts are thus detectable is surely not plausible as a general claim. Although flexible, the cognitive capacities of humans have evolved as a response to a certain concrete environment. There is no reason to think that they are apt for detecting *everything*. Accordingly, some commentators think that there are truths that transcend our cognitive abilities; that is, truths that we will *never* be able to uncover, no matter how much our cognitive position improves. For example, on one prominent view of *vagueness*, vague concepts (such as, "bald") have sharp boundaries. It is just that we cannot obtain knowledge of them (i.e., of whether the concepts apply or not to their borderline cases).[27] Or, to take a more domestic example, no one knows, or indeed *can* know (in a straightforward sense of "can"), that Thales lived an even or odd number of seconds. Still, it may presumably *be* odd.

This possibility might seem to provide a realist with a loophole. For by claiming that *moral* facts are undetectable, he could deny that their existence gives us any reason to expect convergence in ethics, regardless of whether the circumstances are "favorable."

---

25  Of course, an alternative explanation is that Atlantis has existed, but that the evidence has, literally, been washed away.

26  For example, Brink stresses that we would have reason to expect convergence only if "all cognizers were fully informed and fully rational and had sufficient time for deliberation" (*Moral Realism*, 199). It is, presumably, the relevance of the latter consideration that has prompted many commentators to assign special importance to *diachronic* disagreement. In my view, the reason why we may require that the parties to a radical moral disagreement have had sufficient time for deliberation is just that we want to ensure that they are aware of each other's arguments and counterarguments.

27  This is the upshot of the so-called epistemic view, defended by Timothy Williamson in his *Vagueness*, London: Routledge, 1994.

However, an antirealist is likely to insist that this move just takes the realist out of the ashes and into the fire. For, even if *some* facts are undetectable, it is absurd to assume that moral facts are among them. Thus, Thomas Bennigson points out that

to hold that there is an objective fact as to whether wife-shooting is wrong, but that we do not know – and indeed cannot come to know – whether it is wrong is even more counterintuitive than to hold that there is no objective fact of the matter.[28]

Why is the claim that moral truths cannot be known supposed to be so hard to swallow? One possible reason is that it may seem entirely *ad hoc.* According to David Wong, a realist might

say that the disagreement is presently beyond human powers to resolve. But in order to make this more than a cover for there being no fact-of-the-matter for the disagreement to be about, [he] must tell us more about *why* the truth is beyond our reach [. . .][29]

And even if there might be such an explanation in the case of the exact length of Thales's life, Wong is skeptical in the case of ethics. Indeed, this is his main reason for rejecting moral realism.

This means that the argument we are now pondering can be spelled out as follows. A realist cannot account for radical moral disagreement unless he assumes that moral truths are beyond human grasp. However, since that claim in turn is inexplicable, the realist's account is inferior to those available to antirealists. This is why the best explanation of radical moral disagreement assumes that realism is false.

## 3.6. UNDETECTABLE OR UNDERDETERMINED?

One way to respond to this argument is to challenge the alleged absurdity of the claim that moral truths cannot be known. For example, suppose that we are utilitarians and think that the moral rightness of an action depends on its consequences for the total sum of pleasure over pain in the world. Then we can explain why the truth about the rightness of an action is beyond human grasp by appealing to all the familiar problems

---

28 "Irresolvable Disagreement and the Case Against Moral Realism." *Southern Journal of Philosophy* 34 (1996), 411–437, 413. By "wife-shooting," Bennigson alludes to the ways of the Yanomamö Indians.

29 See Wong, *Moral Relativity*, 152 (my italics). On the basis of this argument, Wong rejects absolutism, which is a semantical thesis. However, absolutism is entailed by realism, given the way it has been defined in Chapter 2.

that face everyone who wants to apply utilitarianism to real-life cases (foreseeing the future, making interpersonal comparisons of happiness, and so on).[30] It might be objected that this does not help in the case of *radical* disagreements. For, in such cases, the parties are informed about all relevant nonmoral facts, and these include the facts that are needed in order to apply utilitarianism. But, as I argued in Section 2.8, if we require that the parties to a radical moral disageement have such information, then we have little reason to think that there *are* any radical disagreements.

A weakness of that response, however, is that it relies on a controversial theory in normative ethics. A more promising option, in my view, is to challenge the idea that radical moral disagreement really does commit the realist to think that moral truths cannot be known. Why do they have to assume that moral truths are *undetectable*? Isn't it enough to claim that they are *underdetermined*? That is, isn't it enough to claim that the thinkers who qualify as being parties to a radical moral disagreement (who are in an "optimal cognitive position" relative to the disputed issue) *can* go astray, since their evidence does not logically entail what is the correct answer, which in turn seems perfectly compatible with the idea that the correct answer *can* be known? [31]

For example, let us assume that the parties to a radical moral disagreement proceed in accordance with the idea of reflective equilibrium. According to that idea, roughly, we should confront different sets of moral principles with our considered moral judgments, as well as with certain background theories. If the principles that stand out as the most promising after this scrutiny are still found to conflict with some of the judgments, we are to go "back and forth," sometimes revising the judgments and sometimes the principles. When coherence is achieved, we are justified in accepting both the resulting principles and the revised judgments.[32]

If we assume that the parties reason along this line, we can blame their competing conclusions on differences in their initial moral judgments. Surely, if the method of reflective equilibrium is applied to incompatible starting points, it may yield different conclusions. Or we can blame the

---

30  Crispin Wright mentions this possibility in "Truth in Ethics". Moreover, to invoke a form of consequentialism in the defense of moral realism is part of the strategy Richard Boyd develops in "How To Be a Moral Realist." This is an interesting example of how meta-ethical issues might hinge on ethical ones.

31  I shall return to the distinction hinted at in this paragraph, and discuss its viability in Section 4.6.

32  For detailed descriptions of the method, see Daniels, "Wide Reflective Equilibrium and Theory Acceptance in Ethics," and my *Reflective Equilibrium.*

disagreement on differences regarding the criteria they use in evaluating principles. Maybe the first person assigns greater weight to simplicity, which prompts him to discard principles that the other judges to be promising. That is why some theorists end up utilitarians, whereas others prefer more complex theories.[33]

This explanatory sketch of why people may disagree appears compatible with the assumption that the disagreement is radical.[34] Still, it does not assume that moral facts are *undetectable*. In fact, given this sketch, the question whether there are any moral truths seems entirely irrelevant. Whether people will reach agreement depends solely on whether they have different starting points, or different criteria for evaluating their arguments. So, the sketch does not only allow the realist to deny that the existence of radical moral disagreement commits him to thinking that moral truths are detectable. It also totally undermines the idea that realism can be evaluated with reference to how much agreement it leads us to expect.

It might be objected that the account I have just offered simply reiterates the problem. For if there were moral facts, then people would more often share initial moral beliefs. So, the assumption that there are moral facts does, after all, give us reason to expect more convergence than we in fact encounter. And what explains why people end up disagreeing, even if they have proceeded in accordance with the idea of reflective equilibrium, is the assumption that there are no moral facts. The only way to resist this reasoning is, again, to deny that moral facts are detectable.

However, we can explain why people have different initial moral beliefs without assuming that moral facts are undetectable. Reconsider the research about people's judgments regarding the trolley and footbridge cases mentioned in Chapter 2. The results suggest that a predisposition to make certain moral judgments is hardwired into people's brains, possibly because of natural selection. However, as always with our genetic predispositions, the way they manifest themselves depends on other factors that may differ from culture to culture, and the influence of the predisposition may in the case of some persons be greater than in the case of others, because of individual differences. Someone may point out that this picture does not help the realist, as it invites us to think that we do not need

---

33 What this account does not seem to explain is the fact (if it is a fact) that there is *more* (radical) disagreement in ethics than in the sciences. But maybe one could argue that there are social structures that prompt people to agree in the sciences that are absent in ethics.

34 This depends, however, on which conditions the parties to a radical moral disagreement must satisfy, more precisely. I shall return to that issue in Section 4.4.

to invoke moral facts in explaining our propensity for moral thinking. But then we are back with the first, indirect, version of the argument. So, either way, the inference from the existence of moral disagreement to antirealism is weak.

## 3.7. RELIABILISM

Let us try one final suggestion. The argument that was discussed in the last section was ultimately conceived of as an epistemological argument. Its conclusion was that, if we want to hold on to the idea that our moral questions have objectively true answers, then, in view of the existence of radical moral disagreement, we must assume that their truth cannot be known. In this section, I shall consider another variant on this theme.

In fact, many challenges to moral realism are epistemological. This holds also for Harman's well-known argument. Harman's contention that the best explanation of our moral judgments never assumes that any such judgment is true is supposed to show that moral claims are "immune from observational testing" and that they cannot be "tested against the world." The only way to "test" them, he thinks, is, in accordance with the idea of reflective equilibrium, to examine how well they square with other moral claims that we happen to accept, but such a "test" does not make them justified in a substantial sense, given the empiricist view he favors.[35]

The underlying thought of this reasoning has already been touched upon, namely that we have reason to accept $p$ if $p$ is implied by the best explanation of some state of affairs whose existence can be established independently of our assumptions about $p$. So, because the fact that we have formed a moral judgment can be established independently of our verdict on the judgment, if the best explanation of it assumes that it is true, then our judgment is justified. And the same holds for those further judgments that we are entitled to infer from it. It is worth noting that this means that, if we want to reach the conclusion that no moral judgment is justified, it is not enough to show that no moral judgment is best explained by assuming its truth. We must also show that no moral judgment

---

35 Quine reasons similarly in "On the Nature of Moral Values," reprinted in *Theories and Things*, Cambridge, MA: Harvard University Press, 1981, 55–66. Like Harman, Quine thinks that the difference between science and ethics is that scientific claims, unlike moral claims, are responsive to observation. Thus, he suggests that "[s]cience, thanks to its links with observation, retains some title to a correspondence theory of truth; but a coherence theory is evidently the lot of ethics" (63). For an examination of Quine's argument, see my "Quine on Ethics," *Theoria* 64 (1998), 84–98.

obtains support from any *nonmoral* judgment that satisfies the pertinent condition.[36]

Another problem with Harman's reasoning is that it is based on a view of how we come by our moral judgments that may appear a bit unrealistic. Isn't the idea that we may perceive moral facts, just like we perceive colors, simply unbelievable? In so far as our moral judgments are the result of a process that may render them justified, a more plausible proposal is surely that this is a process of quite complex reasoning.

However, we may formulate the argument without relying on the perceptual view. Thus, we may appeal to *reliabilism*. According to reliabilism, a belief is justified only if it is reliably formed, where this is, roughly, supposed to mean that the belief is the result of a process that yields mostly true beliefs.[37] It might be argued that the existence of radical moral disagreements indicates that there are no such processes in ethics. For, if there were, then there would be a process such that the judgments that are formed in accordance with it largely agree. And the existence of wide disagreement, even among those who are in an optimal cognitive position, indicates that there is no such process.

One of many problems with this argument is reliabilism itself. This may be shown by an argument that is related to the well-known "generality problem."[38] Surely, false beliefs can be justified. Given reliabilism, it follows that false beliefs can be reliably formed. But *when* is a false belief reliably formed? Presumably, it is not enough that it is formed in accordance with some set of conditions such that, say, nearly all of the beliefs formed in accordance with those conditions are true. The reason is that, for any set that contains a number of our beliefs that are true, but also one false belief, we may formulate conditions such that these conditions are satisfied exactly by those beliefs. (For example, we may state the conditions in terms of the times at which they were formed: "Either

---

36  Nicholas Sturgeon makes basically the same point in "Moral Explanations," reprinted in G. Sayre-McCord (ed.), *Essays on Moral Realism*, Ithaca, NY: Cornell University Press, 1988, 229–255. Notice that Sturgeon's suggestion need not conflict with Hume's law. That no nonmoral judgment *n* (by itself) logically entails any moral judgment *m* need not exclude that *m* obtains evidential support from *n*.

37  For a well-known proponent, see A. I. Goldman, "What Is Justified Belief?," in G. Pappas (ed.), *Justification and Knowledge*, Dordrecht: Reidel, 1979, 1–23.

38  The generality problem has been elaborated by Earl Conee and Richard Feldman. See Conee and Feldman, "The Generality Problem for Reliabilism," *Philosophical Studies* 89 (1998), 1–29, and R. Feldman, "Reliability and Justification," *Monist* 68 (1985), 159–174. See also J.L. Pollock, "Reliability and Justified Belief" *Canadian Journal of Philosophy* 14 (1984), 103–114.

formed at $t$ or at $t^{\star}$ or . . .".) So, if we merely require that a belief is formed in accordance with a set of conditions such that nearly all of the beliefs formed in accordance with those conditions are true, we are led to conclude that each and every one of our false beliefs is reliably formed.

This raises the question of how to individuate relevant belief-forming processes. In a plausible version of reliabilism, the mere fact that a belief is formed in accordance with some set of conditions such that most of the beliefs formed in accordance with those conditions are true is not enough. We also should require that it is the fact that they are so formed that *explains* why so many of them are true, presumably as they are the result of a certain mechanism. Now, consider a false belief. This belief is plausibly seen as being the result of the relevant process (rather than of some unreliable process) only if there is a feature of the way it is formed that explains why the mechanism, in this particular case, has malfunctioned. However, if there is such a feature, we cannot avoid the conclusion that the belief is *not* reliably formed, because it is formed under the influence of some disturbing factor. So, either way, the belief is not reliably formed. In other words, reliabilism seems, implausibly, to exclude the possibility of false beliefs being justified. Therefore, any argument that relies on it is questionable.

## 3.8. CONCLUSION

The purpose of this chapter has been to explore the prospects of developing a convincing version of the argument from moral disagreement that is *a posteriori*. The upshot is that the prospects are bleak. All of the proposals that have been considered leave the realist with plenty of room to respond, and none of them strengthens antirealism to any significant extent.

This depends on a number of different factors that have emerged from the discussions in this chapter. One is the fact that we lack an antirealist account of how we come by our moral judgments that has been worked out in enough detail to allow us to say what kind of disagreement it predicts. Another has to do with questions about the conditions under which we are entitled to attribute moral convictions to other thinkers.

For example, I have suggested that radical moral disagreements are problematic for a realist since they challenge the thought that there is a mechanism through which moral facts cause us to believe in them. But if one uses this argument against moral realism, and still thinks that there are areas where we should be realists, one has to show that those areas are *not* plagued with radical disageement. One possibility, which was mentioned in Section 3.3, is to appeal to certain considerations about meaning, reference and interpretation. Thus, one may argue that, in the areas one wants to be realists about, necessarily, if people are disagreeing about the application of a given term *t*, and if the disageement is radical (if none is subject to some cognitive shortcoming), then it is not genuine.

Of course, in order for this proposal to give us a contrast between ethics and those areas, one also has to explain why the strategy in question is not applicable in ethics. The view that it isn't is an implication of the latitude idea, which will be discussed at a later stage. Here, I wish merely to point out that the relevance in the present context of questions about meaning and reference highlights the complex methodological problems that face everyone who wants to confront metaethical theories with empirical data about moral diversity.

There are many recent pleas to the effect that philosophers should get better informed about empirical research, and even pursue empirical research of their own. This is good advice. But in order for it to improve our theorizing we need a better grasp of the methodological status and content of our theories; a grasp that allows us to correctly interpret and make fair assessments of the relevance of the facts that such research might reveal. It must always be remembered that the success of the natural sciences since the scientific revolution does not only depend on the fact that scientists have been better at gathering data and at making observations. It also depends on an improved understanding of how to test theories against these data, for example through the use of mathematics in articulating them, which has made it easier to bring out their observational implications. Unless we in a similar way get a better understanding of the content and status of our philosophical theories, if we want to test them empirically, we don't really know where to look.

# 4

# *The Argument from Inaccessibility*

## 4.1. INTRODUCTION

Realists believe that moral questions have objectively correct answers. According to one of the arguments that were discussed in the last chapter, if there exists radical disagreement over these issues, then a realist must assume, implausibly, that the correctness of those answers cannot be *known*. Given the problems of determining whether any radical moral disagreement actually exists, someone might be tempted to try to squeeze out the same conclusion from the weaker premise that it is at least possible. For example, Crispin Wright has argued that in order to account for the fact that radical moral disagreements cannot be ruled out *a priori*, a realist must assume that moral truths "transcend, even in principle, our abilities of recognition."[1] And that, he insists, is an unreasonable conclusion. Positing undetectable moral truths is as strange as saying that something could be funny even if its funniness evades even the most receptive person.[2]

I call this argument "the argument from epistemic inaccessibility," and it is to this argument the present chapter is devoted. I shall argue that a realist can respond to it. However, one of the responses makes him vulnerable to the argument that is examined in the next chapter ("the argument from ambiguity"). This means that a complete assessment of the argument from inaccessibility must await the discussion that is going to take place there.

---

1   *Truth and Objectivity*, 8f.
2   See, for example, "On Being in Quandary," *Mind* 110 (2001), 45–98, 59.

Crispin Wright is not the only advocate of the argument from inaccessibility.[3] Still, it is his version that I shall focus on, mainly as he has worked it out in more detail than the others.[4]

Wright's aim in his seminal book *Truth and Objectivity* is to find meaningful topics for the debates about realism and antirealism in discourses such as mathematics, ethics and aesthetics. One of the suggestions he pursues is that realism about a discourse is defensible only if it exhibits "Cognitive Command"; that is, only if it is *a priori* that every disagreement that arises in that area (except those that can be attributed to vagueness) involves a cognitive shortcoming of some sort, such as inferential error or ignorance of relevant evidence.[5]

In support of this suggestion, Wright appeals to an analogy between our belief-forming processes and certain devices whose function is to produce representations, such as cameras and fax machines. It is incontestable, he thinks, that if two cameras function properly, and if conditions are suitable, then "they will produce divergent output if and only if presented with divergent input." Analogously, unless every instance of a "divergent output" in *ethics* can be attributed to "divergent input" (differences in evidence), or to malfunction (e.g., inferential error), or to unsuitable conditions (e.g., distraction), we have no reason to think that moral convictions are the products of "a seriously representational mode of function."[6] And because Wright thinks that this condition is not in fact met, he denies that moral views are the products of such a mode.[7]

Wright acknowledges that a realist might respond by saying that every moral disagreement *does* involve a shortcoming, as at least one of its parties

---

3  See also, for example, Alan Goldman, *Moral Knowledge*, London: Routledge, 1988, esp. 153–160, and W. Tolhurst, "The Argument from Moral Disagreement."

4  The argument is developed in *Truth and Objectivity*, esp. 88–94 and 140–68. But see also "Truth in Ethics," and "Realism, Pure and Simple?" The argument is further elaborated in "On Being in Quandary." Notice that Wright's views on the matter have undergone some changes and modifications since *Truth and Objectivity*.

5  For the definition of Cognitive Command, see *Truth and Objectivity*, 144. For the suggestion that it is a necessary (although perhaps not sufficient) condition in order for realism about a discourse to be defensible that it exhibits Cognitive Command, see 148, 162, and 175. For the claim that, even if all *actual* disagreements happen to involve cognitive shortcomings, this does not settle the matter in favor of realism, see "Truth in Ethics," 15.

6  *Truth and Objectivity*, 91–94, and "Truth in Ethics," 13ff.

7  "Truth in Ethics", 15.

is *incorrect*.[8] However, Wright also stresses that if this is the *only* shortcoming a disagreement is supposed to involve, then realists are committed to the view that the truth about the disputed issue may "in principle outreach the efforts of an ordinarily receptive, careful [. . .] thinker."[9] And although he suggests that that idea may be available in other areas, he is skeptical in the case of ethics. Like David Wong, Wright thinks that a realist about an area may appeal to this idea only if he can explain "what it is about its subject matter that potentially makes it so."[10] And Wright thinks that the prospects of providing such an explanation are bleak. This is why he wants to pursue the debate on the assumption that, in ethics, "evidence transcendence is simply not in view."[11]

Wright's argument can accordingly be summarized as a dilemma: realists must assume either that it is *a priori* that every moral disagreement involves some cognitive shortcoming (*other* than the alleged fact that one of its parties is in error about the disputed issue) or that moral truths are inaccessible. Because Wright believes that neither option is acceptable, he rejects realism. That is, he rejects the view that moral judgments are the products of "a seriously representational mode of function."[12]

### 4.3. THE ARGUMENT

Let us take a closer look at the argument. It involves the following premises:

8 For this response, see Timothy Williamson's review article of *Truth and Objectivity* in *International Journal of Philosophical Studies* 1 (1993), 130–44, 139ff.
9 For this reasoning, see *Truth and Objectivity*, 150–7 and "Realism: Pure and Simple?," 333–6. The quoted phrase is from "Truth in Ethics," 9.
10 *Truth and Objectivity*, 152.
11 Truth and Objectivity, 82. As I mentioned in Section 3.6, Wright indicates that the plausibility of this assumption depends on our substantive ethical theory. For example, from a utilitarian point of view, the claim that moral truths are inaccessible may not be objectionable, because, given utilitarianism, the moral status of an action depends on empirical issues that are hard or perhaps impossible to determine. However, notice that that reasoning cannot be invoked in explaining why moral truths are inaccessible for persons that are not ignorant of any nonmoral considerations.
12 Given the way I define "cognitivism" in Chapter 1 (see p. 19), Wright turns therefore out to be a noncognitivist (in spite of the fact that he thinks that ethical sentences are truth apt). However, he is not an expressivist. What status does he assign to moral judgments? He makes an analogy with vagueness. In Wright's view, predications of vague terms to borderline cases are instances of genuine indeterminacy. And he adds: "[W]hat I am suggesting is that discourses in which Cognitive Command fails involve indeterminacy of a structurally similar sort – only not generated [. . .] by semantic vagueness." ("Realism, Pure and Simple?," 334.) In "On Being in Quandary," he calls his position "true relativism."

(i)  The possibility of moral disagreements being radical (that is, such that no cognitive shortcoming is involved) cannot be ruled out *a priori*.

(ii)  If that possiblility cannot be ruled out in the case of a dispute over a given moral issue, and if the issue has a correct answer, then this truth is epistemically inaccessible.

(iii)  There are no epistemically inaccessible moral truths.[13]

This is an attempted *reductio ad absurdum* of moral realism. For realism entails that moral issues have true answers. Thus, given (i) and (ii), a realist is committed to believe something that, according to (iii) is false. However, all premises need clarification.

Let us start with the *scope* of the claim that moral disagreements can be radical. Realists usually concede that there *are* radical moral disagreements, although they stress that these are "few." Some also concede that the proper response to such a case is that there is no correct answer to the issue in dispute (rather than that there is such an answer, but that it is unknowable). This is not to give in to antirealism, however. For realism does not, they stress, entail that *all* moral issues admit of true answers, only that *most* of them do, where those that don't can be attributed to, for example, vagueness.[14] This offers them a way to accept all of the premises. That is, they may point out that all the argument shows is that *some* moral issues have no true answers, which is a conclusion that is perfectly compatible with moral realism.

Vagueness may be invoked also in questioning (iii). There are different views about the nature of vagueness. Everyone agrees that a concept (e.g., bald) is vague to the extent that it allows for borderline cases – that is, cases in which we are in principle unable to determine whether the concept applies or not. However, according to the so-called epistemic theory, there *is* a fact of the matter about the extension of a vague concept also in borderline cases – it is just that we cannot know it.[15] So, given the

---

13  Notice that all of those to whom I have attributed the argument do not accept all the premises. For instance, although Wright accepts all of them, Tolhurst is mainly concerned with (ii). Thus, he points out that his version of the argument "does not aim to show that there are no objective moral truths, only that these truths, if any there be, are epistemically inaccessible" ("The Argument from Moral Disagreement," 611).

14  See, for example, Brink, *Moral Realism*, 202, and Sturgeon, "Moral Disagreement and Moral Relativism," *Social Philosophy and Policy* 11 (1994), 80–115, 95. For similar suggestions, see R. Shafer-Landau, "Ethical Disagreement, Ethical Objectivism and Moral Indeterminacy," *Philosophy and Phenomenological Research*, 54 (1994), 331–44, and "Vagueness, Borderline Cases and Moral Realism," *American Philosophical Quarterly* 32 (1995), 83–96.

15  This theory was mentioned in Chapter 3. A well-known proponent is Timothy Williamson. See his *Vagueness*.

epistemic view, if moral concepts, like other concepts, have borderline cases, the idea that some moral truths are epistemically inaccessible may be defensible.

Presumably, however, realists cannot consistently hold that *all* actions or states of affairs and so forth are borderline cases. So if there is radical disagreement over issues where vagueness cannot be invoked, the possibilities just mentioned do not provide a full response.

In other words, in assessing the argument, we should ignore the cases of radical disagreement that can be attributed to vagueness (as Wright's formulation of Cognitive Command indeed emphasizes). Which cases are those? Obviously, that is a tricky question, and I shall not try to provide a general answer. Instead, I shall approach it on a case-to-case basis.

But the premises need further comments. For example, there are questions about the notion of a radical moral disagreement, and also about the phrase "epistemically inaccessible". The strategy I shall pursue in the rest of the chapter is the following. I will try to find interpretations of these notions such that, when applied consistently to the premises, all of them come out true. This will prove difficult.

### 4.4. TWO CONTROVERSIAL SUGGESTIONS

Let us start with the concept of a radical moral disagreement. A disagreement is radical if and only if it cannot be attributed to some cognitive shortcoming. What counts as such a shortcoming? The concept of a radical disagreement should be construed so as to substantiate the claim that radical disagreements commit realists to the idea that moral truths are epistemically inaccessible. Thus, we should remove any ground for thinking that the cognitive position of the parties to a radical disagreement could somehow be improved.

This means that we should view prejudice, inferential errors, and so on, as shortcomings. We also should include ignorance of relevant nonmoral considerations, which means that we may assume that the parties to a radical disagreement share beliefs about the relevant nonmoral facts.

Are there any other candidates? In this section, I consider two further and possibly more controversial suggestions. I shall argue that, given these suggestions, (i) is false.[16]

According to the first suggestion, just as false nonmoral beliefs may count as a shortcoming, so should false *moral* (background) beliefs.

---

16  The discussion in this section is based on my "Crispin Wright on Moral Disagreement," *Philosophical Quarterly* 48 (1998), 359–65.

Consider a person who accepts a false moral principle. For example, suppose that she thinks that the mere fact that someone is of a specific ethnic origin is a sufficient reason to maltreat him. This may lead her to reach a false verdict about a particular moral judgment (the judgment that a certain act of violence is justified), even if we assume that her nonmoral beliefs are true. Accordingly, a realist may insist that the parties to a radical moral disagreement share not only nonmoral, but also *moral* (background) beliefs.[17]

The second suggestion involves the notion of coherence. Realists think that the verdicts of the parties to a moral disagreement represent conflicting beliefs. Let us say that a belief *p coheres* with a person *a*'s system of beliefs only if there is some (consistent) subset of the rest of *a*'s beliefs such that *p* is at least likely to be true on the assumption that the members of this subset are true, whereas not-*p* does not obtain any such support from *a*'s system, or less.[18] According to the second suggestion, it holds for each of the parties to a radical moral disagreement that his conviction about the disputed issue coheres with his system. The reason for imposing this condition is that a realist may plausibly hold that, unless a moral belief coheres with a person's system, it is not justified for that person, in which case his cognitive position is not optimal.[19]

These suggestions allow a realist to argue that moral disagreements cannot be radical. For, suppose that *a* and *b* are in disagreement over a moral issue, but nevertheless share moral and nonmoral background beliefs. Then it cannot hold for each of them that his verdict coheres with the rest of his beliefs. Both *p* and not-*p* cannot cohere with the *same* set of beliefs (in the indicated sense).

### 4.5. NEUTRAL JUSTIFICATION

Is there something wrong with this reasoning? Remember that realists may stress that at least one of the parties to every moral disagreement is

---

17  Notice that to appeal to the possibility of having false moral (background) judgments is not to beg the question in favor of realism. The argument aims to show that realism should be rejected, since, even if moral issues *were* issues over matters of fact, the correct answers to these issues would be unknowable.

18  The idea that a belief could obtain less support from someone's system than another belief needs clarification. See my *Reflective Equilibrium: An Essay in Moral Epistemology* for some suggestions (esp. Chapter 2).

19  Notice that I assume merely that such coherence is *necessary* for justification, not that it is sufficient.

incorrect. Why does this incorrectness not count as a shortcoming in the relevant sense? According to Wright, the reason is that, if we want to avoid the conclusion that the truths of an area are inaccessible, we have to show that every dispute that arises in the area involves a shortcoming such that we can determine whose it is *independently* of taking a stand in the dispute in question. And this condition does obviously not hold for the fact that one of the parties is incorrect.

Does it hold for my candidates? It holds at least for the suggestion that *incoherence* is a shortcoming. But does it hold for the first suggestion, according to which having false moral (background) beliefs counts as a shortcoming? It certainly seems so. Consider a dispute over a given moral issue. Why would the fact that we have not taken a stand in *that* issue rule out our finding that one of the parties is in error about *other* moral issues?

Maybe Wright would respond by stressing that, in order to ascertain which of the parties has false moral (background) beliefs, we must ultimately consult our *own* moral beliefs, and that something counts as a shortcoming only if we are able to determine that a person is subject to that factor independently of these.[20] However, the idea of such a neutral position from which claims to knowledge could be assessed is questionable. Just as the testing and examination of hypotheses in physics must rely on a portion of current physical theory, the examination of *moral* beliefs relies on our *moral* theories. The idea of a standpoint somehow beyond our system of beliefs from which we could evaluate its members smacks, as Quine would put it, of "first philosophy,"[21] and I am sympathetic to Quine's skepticism toward that idea.[22]

## 4.6. EPISTEMIC INACCESSIBILITY

If we accept the additional suggestions about what counts as a shortcoming considered in the previous section, the argument from inaccessibility fails. But what happens if we reject them? For example, what happens if

---

20  In discussing a similar suggestion, Wright insists that we must be able to decide which of the parties who holds false background theories without having to rely on our own. See *Truth and Objectivity*, 157–68.

21  See, for example, Quine's "Epistemology Naturalized," in *Ontological Relativity*, New York: Columbia University Press, 1969, 69–90.

22  It might be wondered whether such a seemingly relativist view on justification can be combined with a realist view on truth. I defend such a combination in "Coherence and Disagreement," *Philosophical Studies* 65 (1992), 305–17.

we deny that having false moral background beliefs counts as a cognitive shortcoming, and concede that, while the parties to a radical moral disagreement share nonmoral beliefs, they need not share moral background beliefs? In what follows, I shall argue that this allows a realist to provide another, powerful response to Wright's argument. So, in either way, the argument can be met.

Let us turn to the notion "epistemically inaccessible." Wright uses many different phrases to indicate the view he thinks that radical moral disagreement commits a realist to; that moral truths "can transcend all possibility of human knowledge," that they may "transcend, even in principle, our abilities of recognition," and that they may "elude the appreciation even of the most fortunately situated judge."[23]

However, all these phrases are ambiguous in a crucial way. On the one hand, by saying that the truth of some claim $p$ is "transcendent," we could mean that its truth cannot be detected, not even by someone whose cognitive situation couldn't be improved (i.e., who is not subject to any cognitive shortcomings). On the other hand, we could mean that someone *might* fail to apprehend its truth, even if he is optimally equipped from a cognitive point of view.

One may bring out the difference between these claims by construing it as a difference about the scope of the operator "possibly."[24] Both of the parties to a radical disagreement are in an optimal cognitive position (relative to the disputed judgment). By saying that a given truth $p$ is inaccessible, we could mean two different things:

(A) Possibly, it is not the case that everyone who is in an optimal cognitive position relative to $p$ knows that $p$.
(B) It is not the case that, possibly, there is a person who is in an optimal cognitive position relative to $p$ and knows that $p$.[25]

(B) is stronger than (A). That is, (B) implies (A), but not conversely. To see why, consider the traditional view that knowledge is justified true belief. Given this view, and given for example the coherence theory of epistemic justification, it holds for every true belief $p$, that (B) is trivially false, at least if we assume that every true belief could be embedded in a coherent set of beliefs, for, according to coherentism, that is sufficient in

---

23  See *Truth and Objectivity*, 151, 8ff and 58, respectively.
24  What type of modality is at stake here? Whatever kind assumed by the advocates of the argument from inaccessibility.
25  This way of construing the difference has been suggested to me by Richard Holton.

order for a belief to be justified. However, it also follows that, for every statement $p$, (A) is trivially *true*, at least if we make the same assumption about falsehoods.

There are thus two notions of epistemic inaccessibility. In what follows, let us say that, if a truth is inaccessible in the first sense, it is "weakly inaccessible," whereas, if it is inaccessible in the second sense, it is "strongly inaccessible."

When talking about "evidence transcendence," Wright usually seems to have strong inaccessibility or (B) in mind. And this is possibly the notion that is most often employed in debates about realism and antirealism.[26] However, in other passages, he rather seems to talk about weak inaccessibility or (A), as when he suggests that scientific truths are transcendent.[27] In fact, it seems to me that Wright exploits this ambiguity. For, as I shall try to show, (ii) is easier to defend when "epistemically inaccessible" is taken to denote weak rather than strong inaccessibility, while the converse holds for (iii). In any case, the distinction yields two interpretations of (ii) and (iii), and two versions of the argument from inaccessibility. I shall discuss these versions separately, and start with the version focusing on strong inacessibility.

### 4.7. FIRST VERSION

I will take for granted that, if "inaccessible" means "strongly inaccessible," then (iii) – the claim that there are no inaccessible moral truths – cannot plausibly be denied. This should be acceptable to most realists (remember that we ignore cases that can be attributed to vagueness). Indeed, many realists think that realism entails not merely that there are moral truths but that some of these truths are, in fact, known,[28] and much of the discussion of the argument from inaccessibility is pursued under that assumption.[29]

---

26  Wright's discussion of realism is intimately related to Michael Dummett's (see *Truth and Objectivity*, 4ff). In Dummett's case, the relevant notion of "transcendence" seems to be the strong one. See *Truth and Other Enigmas*, London: Duckworth, 1978.

27  See "Realism: Pure and Simple?," 335ff.

28  See Boyd, "How to Be a Moral Realist," 182, and Sturgeon, "Moral Disagreement and Moral Relativism," 95.

29  For example, see Gowans's discussion in "Introduction," in C.W. Gowans (ed.), *Moral Disagreements: Classic and Contemporary Readings*, London: Routledge, 1999. See also Sturgeon's, "Moral Disagreement and Moral Relativism." Sturgeon takes the aim of the argument to be to show that moral issues are "unsettleable," on the basis of the claim that disagreements about them are "unresolvable in principle." It is not clear, however, whether "unsettleable" means that they do not admit of true answers, or just that their answers cannot be uncovered.

But what about (ii)? What about the claim that, if a dispute over a moral issue is radical, and if the issue has a true answer, then it is inaccessible? This claim is less evident. The reason why realists are supposed to be committed to thinking that some moral truths are inaccessible is that they cannot otherwise explain why there may be radical disagreements over them. But that seems already explained by assuming that the truths in question are *weakly inaccessible*. Why go further, and also hold that they are *strongly* inaccessible? In this section, I shall briefly survey some answers to that question. All of them are ultimately rejected.

The plausibility of (ii) might seem to depend on what view we take on knowledge. In what follows, I assume that knowledge is justified true belief (I ignore the Gettier-type counterexamples, as the revisions that these might necessitate have no bearing in the present context). The advocates of the argument from inaccessibility think that we should deny moral realism on the ground that moral judgments cannot constitute knowledge. Because realism entails that moral judgments are beliefs and that such beliefs can be true, the argument for this claim cannot in turn be that moral judgments are not beliefs, or that they cannot be true (since that would beg the question). Rather, the argument must be that they cannot be *justified*. Why is radical moral disagreement supposed to show that moral judgments cannot be justified?

Consider the following reasoning. If two persons disagree over a moral belief *p*, and if their disagreement is radical, then, from an optimal cognitive position, *p* is as likely to be true as its negation. But this is just to say that *neither p nor* not-*p* is justified, as a belief, to use Wright's phrase, "does not count as justified [. . .] unless the case in its favor dominates anything that counts in favour of its negation."[30]

This argument assumes that justification is a property of propositions. By contrast, I assume that the relevant concept of justification applies to *beliefs*, and that it should, accordingly, be relativized to persons. I also assume that different persons may be justified in believing different things, depending on differences in epistemic outlook, and so on.

Given that assumption, we must rephrase the argument. Suppose that *a* believes *p* while *b* believes not-*p* and that their disagreement is radical. It may be held that, as both these persons are in an optimal, and therefore *equally good* cognitive position relative to the disputed proposition, their beliefs are either both justified or both *not* justified. It also might be held

---

30   *Truth and Objectivity*, 39.

72

that if $a$'s (or $b$'s) belief is not justified, then, given that $a$ (like $b$) is in an *optimal* cognitive position relative to $p$, nor is anybody else's. These two assumptions imply that if *anyone's* belief about $p$ is justified, both $a$'s and $b$'s beliefs are justified. But, since both beliefs cannot be justified, no belief about $p$ is justified.

Why cannot both $a$'s and $b$'s beliefs be justified? Obviously, the claim that both $a$'s and $b$'s beliefs are justified implies that a *false* belief could be justified. Indeed, it might seem to imply that false beliefs could be *maximally* justified, at least given that there is no "higher" justification than that which can be achieved by someone who meets the conditions of the parties to a radical disagreement. And this might be problematic.

But is it? Of course, if (maximal) justification is taken to imply truth, then we have a problem. But, given any plausible view on justification, that is not so. Moreover, in an argument against moral realism – the view that moral judgments can be true independently on whether we can prove that they are true – to appeal to such a claim would beg the question.

Let us instead consider a suggestion by William Tolhurst. Tolhurst suggests that if a person is justified in holding a belief $p$, and another person is justified in holding not-$p$, then there must be some epistemically relevant difference between them.[31] Perhaps this is the problem with the claim that both $a$'s and $b$'s beliefs are justified: there is no relevant difference.

But isn't there? The fact that the disagreement is radical rules out that they differ in their nonmoral beliefs. But it does not (given the present interpretation of "cognitive shortcoming") exclude that they differ in their moral (background) beliefs. For example, their moral background beliefs may differ in such a way that $p$ may be logically implied by (some consistent subset of) the rest of $a$'s beliefs, while not-$p$ is logically implied by (some consistent subset) of the rest of $b$'s beliefs. This may be so, even if they share nonmoral beliefs, and even if some of those beliefs function as essential members of those subsets. Surely, that is a crucial difference, given any viable theory of justification.

In other words, there is nothing absurd about the conclusion that there are moral judgments such that people can be justified in giving conflicting verdicts on them. In fact, a realist should be *happy* to accept such a claim. For, if it holds for any moral belief $p$ that both $p$ and not-$p$ may be justified, then it follows that any *true* moral belief may be justified, and hence that any moral truth *could* be known!

31   "The Argument from Moral Disagreement," 611.

So, if "inaccessible" is taken to denote strong inaccessibility, then a realist can deny (ii). That is, he can deny that the possibility of a moral disagreement being radical shows that the truth about the disputed issue cannot be known. However, if it is taken to mean weak inaccessibility, then (ii) cannot be denied. Suppose that a given moral judgment is true, and that two persons are in disagreement over it. Given that none of them is subject to some cognitive shortcoming, it follows that a person *could* fail to apprehend a moral truth, even if he is optimally placed from a cognitive point of view.

What about (iii)? Is it *implausible* to hold that moral truths are weakly inaccessible? The problem with the claim that moral truths are inaccessible was supposed to be that it couldn't be explained. However, to explain why a truth $p$ is *weakly* inaccessible is to explain why a person may form an erratic belief about $p$, even if he is in an optimal cognitive position relative to $p$. And that doesn't seem particularly difficult.

One way to explain why someone has formed an erratic belief is to show that it was reasonable for the believer to accept it, given his particular outlook and evidence. If your friend has forgotten to tell you about his twin brother, it is understandable if you falsely believe that your friend has become rude when the brother doesn't answer your "Hi" when you meet him on the street. Now, the fact that a person $a$ is in an optimal cognitive position relative to a true moral belief $p$ does not rule out that it is rational for him to deny $p$. For suppose that not-$p$ coheres with the rest of $a$'s beliefs. In particular, suppose that not-$p$ is *implied* by the rest of $a$'s beliefs (while $p$ does not obtain any such support). Since this means that not-$p$ is supported by other claims $a$ believes to be true, it makes it reasonable for $a$ to accept not-$p$, even if it is false.

Of course, the assumption that not-$p$ is false and that not-$p$ coheres with the rest of $a$'s beliefs, suggests that $a$ holds *other* moral beliefs that are false, given the truth of his nonmoral beliefs. (This is trivially true if not-$p$ is *implied* by the rest of $a$'s beliefs). But that is not excluded by the fact that he is in an optimal cognitive position relative to $p$, since, as we assumed earlier, having false moral background beliefs does not count as a shortcoming. Moreover, if it holds for each of those errors that it coheres with his system, all of them are explicable.[32]

---

32  Of course, each of his beliefs cannot be *entailed* by the rest, but this does not exclude that each of them *coheres* with the rest.

In other words, a realist could argue that it holds for any moral belief, just as it holds for other beliefs, that yet further beliefs may conspire to make it rational to accept it, even if it is false. So, any moral error is potentially explicable, and the type of explanation I have sketched does not commit a realist to any extravagant assumptions about the nature of moral facts.

## 4.9. CAN MORAL DISAGREEMENTS BE RADICAL?

But maybe this is too quick. Notice that the present proposal presupposes that it could be reasonable for an optimally placed person to stubbornly hold on to a false belief, even if he recognizes that others think differently, and even if he acknowledges that they (too) are in an optimal cognitive position (we assume now that the fact that he is "optimally placed" means that he has that information). This is a questionable presupposition. In my view, it is plausible to insist that, if one acknowledges that someone else thinks differently, then one is justified in holding on to one's own belief to any significant extent only if one can somehow explain *why* one's opponent has reached a wrong conclusion. And many potential explanations are ruled out by the assumption that the disagreement is radical.

For example, if someone is in radical moral disagreement with someone else, then he cannot attribute the opponent's (alleged) error to bias or to inferential mistakes or to some similar shortcoming. Perhaps he can blame it on the (alleged) fact that the opponent started his reasoning from false moral initial beliefs. But there is something arbitrary about such a move. Why believe that one's opponent's starting points are false whereas one's own are not, especially if one realizes that one's opponent is not in any *other* respects less well equipped from a cognitive point of view? The concern here is that, when one is in radical disagreement, any attempt to explain away the other's verdict makes one vulnerable to the possibility that the same strategy could be used against oneself!

There is yet another objection to the present proposal. I noted earlier that if we explain why a person holds a false moral belief on the ground that it coheres with his system, then, given that he is in an optimal cognitive position, we must assume that many of his other moral beliefs are also false. For, if he is in an optimal cognitive position, all his nonmoral beliefs are true. And a false belief cannot cohere with a system (to any significant extent) unless it contains many *other* false beliefs. However, attributing so much moral error may seem desperate and *ad hoc*.[33]

33  This is stressed by David Brink. See *Moral Realism*, 209.

I shall therefore concede that there is no believable explanation of why moral truths are inaccessible, even if we assume that "inaccessible" means "weakly inaccessible." That is, I shall concede that, if there are radical moral disagreements then a moral realist has to attribute inexplicable errors. This means that we must return to the first premise of the argument: *can* moral disagreements be radical? In the rest of this section, I shall develop an argument to the effect that, if a realist concedes that radical moral disagreements forces him to attribute inexplicable errors, or indeed *because* he makes this concession, he can argue that moral disagreements cannot be radical.

Reconsider the schema in Chapter 2:

|  | Radical | Nonradical |
|---|---|---|
| Genuine | (1) | (2) |
| Merely apparent | (3) | (4) |

(1) is the crucial square. Radical disagreements do not undermine realism unless they are genuine. However, according to the argument I am about to develop, if it is granted that realists have to conceive of errors made by people who are in an optimal cognitive position as inexplicable, they could argue that there is a tension between the assumption that a moral disagreement is genuine and the assumption that it is radical. That is, they could argue that the claim that an apparent moral disagreement is radical rules out that it is genuine, which means that it is indeed *a priori* that (1) is empty and that all radical disagreements belong to (3). Thus, in either way, the argument from inaccessibility can be met. If errors made by the parties to a radical moral disagreement are inexplicable, then the realist can reject (i). If not, he can reject (iii).

### 4.10. THE SEMANTIC MOVE

Suppose that we disagree with someone over an ethical sentence *s*. According to the definition stated in Section 2.3, this dispute represents a genuine disagreement if "his" *s* can be translated with ours. Realists think that a genuine moral disagreement constitutes a conflict of beliefs.

Thus, realism entails that "his" *s* can be translated with ours only if we use *s* to express the same belief (beliefs with the same content), since our dispute otherwise does not constitute a conflict of beliefs. So, if it could be shown that the claim that the dispute is radical entails that we use *s* to express *different* beliefs, this allows a realist to deny that genuine moral disagreements can be radical. This is the possibility (which was hinted at already in Section 2.9 and again in 3.3) that I shall explore.

At this point, we confront issues about belief attribution and interpretation. According to the Davidsonian view to which I have kept returning, we interpret a speaker correctly only if we represent him as agreeing with us about most matters. This is the upshot of his "principle of charity." The principle of charity has often been criticized on the ground that it may sometimes be more appropriate to attribute beliefs with which we disagree. For instance, Richard Grandy thinks that it is "better to attribute [. . .] an explicable falsehood than a mysterious truth."[34] And Steven Lukes gives the following advice: "Count them [the speakers] right unless we can"t explain their being right or can better explain their being wrong.'[35] However, the principle does not exclude the attribution of error altogether. Indeed, Davidson has often insisted that the very *point* of the principle is to "make meaningful disagreement possible."[36]

One possible motive for attributing false beliefs is to avoid making our theory too complex.[37] Suppose that we find that a speaker accepts *s* when and only when it's raining (nearby). Then we try for a theory of interpretation that implies that *s* is true (in the speaker's idiolect) if and only if it's raining (nearby). Now, suppose that we at some later point find that the speaker accepts the sentence when it is *not* raining. In this case, we have a choice. Either to revise the theory so that it ascribes a meaning to *s* that makes it true also in this case. Or to hold on to our initial theory. If we choose to revise it, we must revise its axioms. If these revisions yield a more complicated theory than the initial one, this is a reason to hold on to the initial theory, and, thus, for attributing errors.

However, Davidson has stressed that such considerations justify attributing error only if the error is *explicable*; that is, only if we can explain

34 "Reference, Belief and Meaning," *Journal of Philosophy* 70 (1973), 439–452, 445.
35 "Relativism in its Place," in M. Hollis and S. Lukes (eds.), *Rationality and Relativism*. Oxford: Blackwell, 1982, 261–305, 262. Several others make similar remarks. See, for example, Lewis, "Radical Interpretation," 112, and D. Follesdal, "The Status of Rationality Assumptions in Interpretation and in the Explanation of Action," *Dialectica* 36 (1982), 301–316.
36 *Inquiries*, 196.
37 Ibid.

why the speaker mistakenly believes that it is raining (say, by assuming that he sits inside, hears water falling on the roof, but is unaware of the fact that the water stems from some gardener's doings). Thus, on this view, to attribute true beliefs is the default position, and in order to attribute an erratic belief we need a special reason, in the form of an explanation of how the interpretee has acquired it, presumably in terms of some cognitive shortcoming, such as misleading evidence or non-standard perceptual conditions. Consider the following passages:

If you see a ketch sailing by and your companion says, "Look at that handsome yawl," you may be faced with a problem of interpretation. One natural possibility is that your friend has mistaken a ketch for a yawl, and has formed a false belief. But if his vision is good and his line of sight favourable it is even more plausible that he does not use the word "yawl" quite as you do, and has made no mistake at all about the position of the jigger on the passing yacht.[38]

And:

When we find a difference inexplicable, that is, not due to ignorance or confusion, the difference is not genuine: put from the point of view of an interpreter, finding a difference inexplicable is a sign of bad interpretation.[39]

In other words, on the present view, if two persons disagree over a given sentence, and if the assumption that they use the sentence to express the same belief implies that one of them has made an inexplicable error, we should reject that assumption. Now, moral realism entails that at least one of the parties to any genuine moral disagreement is in error. Given that it would be impossible to explain why one of the parties to a *radical* moral disagreement is in error, as the argument from inaccessibility assumes, the advice in question allows a realist to argue that no (genuine) moral disagreement can be found to be radical. That is, he can appeal to this advice in order to argue that it *is* indeed *a priori* that every (genuine) moral disagreement involves cognitive shortcomings.[40]

---

38   Ibid.
39   "Objectivity and Practical Reason," 25. See also *Inquiries*, 196.
40   Notice that, if this reasoning is sound, it reveals Wright's analogy between our belief-forming processes and cameras as seriously misleading. The reason is that we can decide whether two photographs differ independently of determining whether there is "divergent input" or "unsuitable conditions." What a person believes, on the other hand, is *not* directly observable. Rather, the concept of belief is a highly *theoretical* concept, and whether we can find that there is a genuine disagreement is not independent of whether we can provide a plausible explanation of it (in terms of divergent input or unsuitable conditions).

There are many ways to respond to the above reasoning. For example, it might be objected that, even if it counts against a scheme of interpretation that it represents a speaker as having made an inexplicable error, other considerations (such as its degree of simplicity) may compensate for this and justify our sticking to the theory. We may also, of course, question the entire approach to meaning and interpretation on which it relies.

Objections of this type raise intricate questions in philosophy of language, and I shall return to them in the next chapter. Here, I wish merely to stress that, if we dismiss the reasoning sketched above, we are left with a certain enigma, namely to explain how it could be shown for *any* discourse that it is *a priori* that no disagreement that arises in that discourse is radical. Remember that we are looking for a *special* reason to be antirealists about ethics. Obviously, if there is *no* discourse where the possibility of radical disagreement can be ruled out, the (alleged) fact that it cannot be ruled out in ethics gives us no such reason.

This observation applies particularly well to Wright. According to Wright, one possible ground for being a realist about a discourse is that its truths are inaccessible. Physics provides (unlike ethics) an example.[41] However, a central theme in *Truth and Objectivity* is that there are discourses in which this option is ruled out but where it is *still* reasonable to be a realists.[42] After all, if the contrast between areas that should be construed realistically and those that should not only is a matter of whether its truths may be held to be inaccessible, there would be no point in stating the contrast in terms of disagreement (through Cognitive Command). Now, the only *other* way to show that we are entitled to be realists about a discourse is to show that it is *a priori* that none of the disagreements that arise in it is radical. So, Wright is committed to thinking that there are some discourses for which this condition holds. But how could that be shown? What I have done, in effect, is to suggest an answer. So, if Wright denies that this move is legitimate, he owes us an alternative. But no alternative has been offered, and, as far as I can see, there is none.

Another line of criticism against the semantic move is to argue that, although the views on belief attribution on which it relies might be applicable in other areas, they are not applicable in the case of ethics.

41   See "Realism: Pure and Simple?," 335.
42   See, for example, 5, 82, and 162.

Why hold that view? Obviously, the reason cannot be that moral views, unlike other views, are not "seriously representational." For that would beg the question. Rather, we must appeal to some other, independent, reason.

Notice that what we are looking for here is, in effect, a justification of the latitude idea; the thesis about when to attribute moral views that I have mentioned several times before. For one feature of the latitude idea is, precisely, that it allows us to find ourselves in genuine moral disagreement also with people whose differing verdicts cannot be explained away with reference to some cognitive shortcoming. That is, the latitude idea allows us to translate someone's "morally right" or "just" with ours, even if our differences as to how apply these terms cannot be attributed to such deficiencies.

I shall defend the latitude idea in Chapter 6, but part of its plausibility may be brought out through considering another objection to the semantic move. According to this objection, the conclusion that the parties to a radical disagreement simply talk past each other doesn't help the realist, because it squares badly with the fact that it may still exhibit the *appearance* of genuine disagreement. Hare and Blackburn and other antirealists think that this is where it really itches when it comes to realism and disagreement, and this is also the upshot of the argument from ambiguity which is to be discussed in the next chapter. Given the relevance of this argument to the evaluation of the semantic move, a complete assessment of the argument from inaccessibility must await what is happening there.

Let me consider one final, but related, objection. David Wong is one of the advocates of the argument from inaccessibility. He thinks that it refutes realism, or more specifically its *semantical* component. However, he does not abandon cognitivism altogether, but merely the *absolutist* version to which realism is committed (roughly, the view according to which all thinkers, regardless of which language they speak or which cultural group they belong to, attribute the same property to an action by judging it morally right or morally wrong). Instead, Wong advocates a form of *relativism*, according to which moral judgments contain a reference to the system of rules that applies to, or is accepted by, the speaker of the sentence. This theory allows us to say that a sentence $s$ of a speaker $a$'s idiolect can be translated with an ethical sentence of our idiolect, even if these sentences have different truth conditions in our respective idiolects, just as a Frenchman's "Je suis ici" could be translated with my "I am here" even if those sentences express beliefs with different truth conditions for me and him.[43]

Now, recall the characterization of a genuine moral disagreement offered in Section 2.3. According to this characterization, if we think, say, that the death penalty should be abolished, then someone else disagrees with us if he rejects a sentence *s* whose content can correctly be given by our sentence "The death penalty should be abolished." Since Wong's theory does not rule out our translating *s* with "The death penalty should be abolished," even if those sentences have different truth conditions, then it allows us to concede that radical moral disagreements involve no conflicts of belief and still insist that those disagreements may be genuine. That may seem to be an advantage of his theory, in view of the kind of worries raised by the advocates of the argument from ambiguity. I shall return to this discussion in Chapter 5.

## 4.12. CONCLUSION

The argument from epistemic inaccessibility is an attempt to refute moral realism through a *reductio*. It aims to show that realists, in response to radical moral disagreement, must assume, implausibly, that moral truths are epistemically inaccessible.

I have argued that a realist can respond to this argument by distinguishing between two senses of "epistemic inaccessibility" – *strong* and *weak*. Roughly, a truth *p* is strongly inaccessible if it is *impossible* to obtain knowledge of it, even for a person who is optimally equipped from a cognitive point of view, whereas it is weakly inaccessible if it is possible for such a person to fail to apprehend it. That is, I have argued that radical moral disagreement at best commits a realist to the latter view, and that this does not provide a reason to reject realism.

Maybe I am wrong about this. Maybe the claim that moral truths are weakly inaccessible is also objectionable, since realists cannot explain why they are thus inaccessible. I also have suggested that, if we concede this

---

43  Maybe Wong himself would deny this view about translation (and the view that a moral disagreement can be genuine even if there is no conflict of beliefs). For the details of Wong's theory, see his *Moral Relativity*, esp. Chapters 3–6. Alan Goldman also takes (his version of) the argument from inaccessibility to support a form of relativism (see *Moral Knowledge*, esp. Chapter 4), although his version differs from Wong's. Goldman wants to explain moral truth in terms of coherence, and this is what is supposed to yield relativism, rather than the fact that ethical terms have different referents for different speakers.

point, a realist could provide another response. For it might be argued that, given certain meaning-theoretical views, this allows a realist to argue that radical moral disagreements are merely apparent. Surely, a realist is likely to react by saying "with advocates like that, who needs adversaries?" But why? What is it about that move that makes it so counterintuitive? This is the question to which we now turn.

# 5

# *The Argument from Ambiguity*

## 5.1. INTRODUCTION

At several points in the preceding discussion, I have toyed with the idea that a realist can dismiss objections that appeal to radical moral disagreement by arguing that the parties to such disputes really talk past each other. In other words, they can insist that when one of the parties says that an action is permissible and another denies this, they are not really contradicting each other, since "permissible," for them, refers to different properties. In spite of its perhaps striking counterintuitiveness, some writers of a realist inclination have in fact made this move. They have argued that, given certain plausible ideas about meaning and belief attribution, the extent of genuine moral disagreement is exaggerated.[1]

Many antirealists go along with this. That is, they agree that, under certain circumstances, ethical sentences express different beliefs for different speakers.[2] However, they deny that this conclusion strengthens the realist's position. On the contrary, it seriously weakens it, and the reason is, precisely, that it *does* commit realists to regarding many moral disagreements as merely verbal. In their view, such an implication is absurd, which is shown by the fact that many of the relevant disputes will still exhibit the *appearance* of a genuine conflict. They conclude that, to have a genuine moral disagreement is not to accept conflicting propositions, and to have

---

1  See D. Cooper, "Moral Relativism;" S. Hurley, "Objectivity and Disagreement;" R. D. Milo, "Moral Deadlock," *Philosophy* 61 (1986), 453–71; and J. Stout, *Ethics After Babel.*

2  At least if we assume that they express beliefs at all. With this addition, the claim in question becomes hypothetical and could be accepted also by expressivists who (implausibly) deny that ethical sentences express beliefs.

a moral conviction is not to have a belief. This argument – "the argument from ambiguity" – provides the focus of the present chapter.[3] I shall argue that it does indeed undermine realism.

Notice that this conclusion is relevant also to the assessment of the argument from inaccessibility. The reason is that it blocks one possible response to it. Indeed, the argument from inaccessibility and the argument from ambiguity can be combined to form a dilemma. That is, it could be argued that realists, in response to radical moral disagreement, must *either* assume that moral truths are epistemically inaccessible *or* that such disagreements are merely apparent. If both of these assumptions are implausible, realists are in trouble.[4]

## 5.2. CANNIBALS AND PRIESTS

According to the argument from ambiguity, there are disputes over ethical sentences that do not involve conflicts of beliefs. How could that claim be established? Or better, how could it be established in a neutral way? After all, realists are likely to insist that there *is* some fact over which the parties to any dispute over an ethical sentence disagree, namely a *moral* fact. Indeed, that may seem as a trivial consequence of the realist doctrine that ethical terms refer to "real properties" and that sentences that predicate such terms have truth conditions.

Still, the advocates of the argument think that they are able to provide independent support for the claim in question. The reason is that one may accept that ethical terms refer to "real properties" and still deny that speakers use them to refer to the *same* properties. Obviously, if they use them to refer to different properties, then disputes over their application need not represent conflicts of belief. Speakers may disagree over "Peter

---

3  Nicholas Sturgeon regards this as "a standard argument for noncognitivism" ("Contents and Causes," *Philosophical Studies* 61 [1991], 19–37, 20). It can be attributed to expressivists such as Simon Blackburn, Richard Hare, and Charles Stevenson. See Blackburn, *Spreading the Word*, 168, and "Just Causes," 4; Hare, *The Language of Morals*, 148ff; and "A 'Reductio Ad Absurdum' of Descriptivism," in S. Shanker (ed.), *Philosophy in Britain Today*, London: Croom Helm, 1986, 118–36; and Stevenson, *Facts and Values*, 48–51. See also Darwall et al., "Toward *Fin de Siècle* Ethics," 185; and Loeb, "Moral Realism and the Argument from Disagreement," *Philosophical Studies* 90 (1998), esp. 292–301.
4  The intimate relationship between the arguments is noted by Loeb. See his "Moral Realism and the Argument from Disagreement." However, notice that the advocates of the argument from ambiguity usually believe that realists are committed to the conclusion that many moral disagreements are merely apparent independently of whether they need to appeal to this view in response to the argument from inaccessibility.

is on his way to the bank." But if they use "bank" to refer to different things, their statements are not incompatible.

When is it plausible to think that two persons use an ethical term to refer to different properties? This depends on our views on reference. The advocates of the argument usually appeal to the fact that people systematically apply them differently, and on the basis of different kinds of considerations. Utilitarians assign weight to consequences regarding well-being, Kantians to intentions. Nozickians focus on the way a distribution has emerged, egalitarians on the way it is structured. Given many views on reference and belief attribution, diversity of this kind undermines co-reference.[5] Of course, in the case of nonmoral contexts, differences in language use of this kind seldom occur, for the obvious reason that to speak like others brings various benefits. Someone who systematically applies "red" to blue things is bound to be misunderstood. However, ethical terms provide a noteworthy exception, which is exactly what the advocates of the argument from ambiguity try to exploit.

We also may imagine other facts about our use of ethical terms that, given other theories of reference, yield the same conclusion. I shall shortly examine some variations of that kind. Here, I wish merely to note that neither the facts about people's use of ethical terms to which the advocates of the argument from ambiguity appeal, nor the views on reference on which they rely, seem to beg any questions. This is why the argument is potentially powerful. It also should be noted that the argument applies equally well to naturalist and nonnaturalist forms of moral realism. For the nature of the properties to which ethical terms are supposed (by realists) to refer is irrelevant to whether the differences in use on which the argument focuses yield, together with the general theories of meaning and reference on which it relies, the conclusion that speakers refer to different properties with the terms in question.

Richard Hare was possibly the first to launch the argument from ambiguity. In a famous passage in *The Language of Morals*, he imagines

---

5  Here and elsewhere, I formulate the premise of the argument from ambiguity in terms of *properties*, and I talk of terms as *referring* to properties. Skeptics about the existence of properties may find this talk awkward. However, it should be noted that the premise could just as well be formulated in terms of truth conditions or propositions or beliefs. For example, by saying that a term refers to different properties for different persons, I mean that their predications of that term express different beliefs (beliefs with different contents). Notice also that, by saying that a speaker "assigns" a referent (or meaning) to a term, I do not wish to indicate that the referent (or meaning) a term has in a speaker's idiolect can be determined in some simple way by his own will. It is just a convenient way of saying that the term *has* that referent (or meaning) in that speaker's idiolect.

a missionary who lands on a "cannibal island." The missionary finds that the "cannibals" use "good," just as he, as "the most general adjective of commendation." But he also finds that they apply it differently. The natives apply it to persons who are "bold and burly and collect more scalps than the average," whereas the missionary applies it to those who are "meek and gentle and do not collect large quantities of scalps." According to Hare, these differences rule out the view that the missionary and the cannibals assign the same "descriptive" meaning to "good."[6] They do *not*, however, rule out that their disputes constitute genuine moral disagreements.

But maybe we don't have to go to so far as to cannibals. Simon Blackburn has suggested that it is enough to turn to priests. Suppose that a priest and a utilitarian disagree over the sentence "Contraception should be abolished." The utilitarian rejects this sentence, because he believes that contraception promotes happiness, whereas the priest embraces it, on the ground that contraception is "against the wishes of the creator of the universe." According to Blackburn, this difference indicates that, insofar as the sentence is used to express beliefs at all, the parties use it to express different beliefs. Therefore, a realist must regard the dispute as merely apparent. An expressivist, by contrast, "locates the disagreement where it should be, in the clash of attitudes towards contraception."[7]

C. L. Stevenson introduces a dynamic element.[8] Suppose that two persons discuss whether to attribute "just" to a particular law. Suppose, moreover, that they do not "disagree in belief," and, accordingly, that they use the term to refer to different properties. For example, suppose that the first person, who argues that the law is just, expresses the proposition that it will lead to consequences X and Y, whereas the second person, who denies that the law is just, expresses the proposition that it will not lead to consequences Y and Z. As these propositions are compatible, they need not have incompatible beliefs. From a realist point of view, this means that their dispute is merely apparent. But that is the wrong conclusion. For

the first man will feel, even after the discrepancy in terminology is clearly realized, that he has been opposed from the very beginning. He will feel the need of refuting his opponent's statement as though this was necessary to support his own.[9]

---

6  *Language of Morals*, 146–9.
7  *Spreading the Word*, 168. See also "Just Causes," 4.
8  In this context, Stevenson says: "[My meta-ethical views] center less on my conception of meaning than on my conception of agreement and disagreement," *Facts and Values*, 170.
9  *Facts and Values*, 49.

So, even if the parties were to *recognize* that they use "just" to refer to different properties, they would continue to "feel opposed" and to pursue the discussion. By contrast, if two persons disagree over "Peter is on his way to the bank," but use "bank" to refer to different things, they would soon realize this, and their dispute would wither. This suggests that realists give a wrong account of what goes on in moral disagreements.

## 5.3. THE AMBIGUITY CLAIM

Let us say that disputes over ethical sentences that cannot be construed as conflicts of beliefs satisfy *the ambiguity condition*. Before examining the argument more closely, I shall make some preliminary comments.

First, the fact that a dispute satisfies the ambiguity condition implies that the parties assign different truth conditions to the sentence in dispute (in so far as they assign truth conditions to it at all). Does this in turn imply that they assign different *meanings* to it, or to the term predicated by the sentence? Well, there is a (non-Fregean) sense of "meaning" in which two persons may assign the same meaning to a sentence even if their utterances of it have different truth conditions. Consider "I am hungry." When *I* utter this sentence, I express a different belief (a belief with a different truth condition) as compared to when *you* utter it. However, it may still seem right to say that it has the same meaning for you and me. This might indicate that the term "ambiguity" is ill-chosen. However, if we keep in mind that the argument merely assumes that disputes that satisfy the ambiguity condition need not involve conflicts of beliefs, there should be no problem.

Second, there is a question about the scope of the claim that there are disputes that satisfy the ambiguity condition. Does the argument require that it is *actually* satisfied by certain disputes, or is it enough that we can imagine such cases? The advocates of the argument seem to take the latter stance, given their appeal to thought experiments, and I shall pursue the discussion under that assumption.[10] We'll get a clearer picture of whether this is plausible when we have considered more closely *why* it is supposed to be problematic for realism that it must construe such disputes as merely apparent.

Third, notice that *any* plausible theory of reference or belief attribution entails that there are *some* circumstances under which a dispute over an

---

10  For example, Michael Smith, who uses the argument against Boyd's version of realism, says that the problem is that Boyd's theory "leaves open the *possibility* that we should explain such disagreements away" (*The Moral Problem*, 205, my italics).

ethical sentence need not involve a conflict of beliefs. This is a consequence of the trivial fact that what property a term refers to in a speaker's idiolect, and what truth conditions he assigns to sentences that predicate the term, is a contingent matter. Therefore, the fact that there are such circumstances cannot by itself be a problem for realism. It is a problem only if those disputes have certain other features; features that render this conclusion implausible. Thus, they must in various ways display an *appearance* of a genuine disagreement, in that each of the parties "feel opposed" to the other, and "feel the need of refuting his opponent's statement as though this were necessary to support his own," and so on.

The plan of the rest of the chapter is as follows. The argument from ambiguity involves two main premises. According to the first, there are (or can be) disputes over ethical sentences where the parties "feel opposed" to each other, and so on, but that realists have to construe as merely apparent. According to the second, to construe such disagreements as merely apparent is incorrect or implausible. The argument for the first premise appeals to the thesis that such disputes satisfy the ambiguity condition. I shall call this thesis "the ambiguity claim," and it will be defended in Sections 5.4 through 5.7. The second premise is defended in Sections 5.8 and 5.9. In Section 5.10, finally, some concluding remarks are made.

### 5.4. CHARITY AND AMBIGUITY

The stories about the missionary and the cannibals, and about the priests and the utilitarians, are meant to illustrate that people apply ethical terms differently, and on the basis of radically different considerations. This in turn is supposed to show that they use the terms (if at all) to refer to different properties. Why?

Such differences undermine co-reference only if we assume the reference of a term in a speaker's idiolect or language, and the truth conditions of sentences that predicate it, are in some way determined by its *use*. We must also, presumably, assume that the reference is determined by the speaker's *own* use.

For example, consider again Davidson's principle of charity. This principle entails that a theory of interpretation is viable only if the truth conditions it assigns to the speaker's sentences are such that the sentences held true by the speaker *are*, by and large, true (by our lights). So, we have reason to deny that a person who systematically applies, say, "red" differently (e.g., to blue, and only blue, things) uses this term to refer to the same property as we do, because we otherwise are led to conclude he is in massive error. In order for an argument that appeals to the principle of charity to be convincing, however, we need some justification of it. Why should we accept it? Let us briefly address that question.

In trying to defend the principle of charity, Davidson sketches various hypothetical cases where it intuitively seems to give the right verdict. Thus, we may imagine a person who disagrees with us about some particular feature of the earth (e.g., its form). But if we suspect that he disagrees with us also about many other of its features (that it is inhabited, etc.) we are soon led to question whether we have reason to attribute any beliefs about the earth to this person at all. Or as Davidson puts it:

Beliefs are identified and described only within a dense pattern of beliefs. I can believe a cloud is passing before the sun, but only because I believe there is a sun, that clouds are made of water vapour, that water can exist in liquid or gaseous form; and so on. [. . .] No particular list of further beliefs is required [. . .] but some appropriate set of related beliefs must be there.[11]

However, these cases are meant to illustrate a more elaborate argument. Like Wittgenstein, and Quine, Davidson is sympathetic to the idea that language is an intrinsically *social* phenomenon.[12] In Davidson's view, this idea implies that it is in principle possible for someone to interpret someone else's utterances correctly solely on the basis of information that, on the one hand, is publicly accessible, and, on the other hand, neither presupposes prior knowledge of the meanings of his utterances, nor of the contents of his beliefs. The kind of information Davidson has in mind is information about which sentences the speaker holds true (and false) and about the conditions under which he accepts (and rejects) them; that is, the evidence available to a "radical interpreter."[13] It may be difficult, however, to see how we can get from such information to knowledge about the meanings of the speaker's sentences. It is here that the principle of charity comes into the picture.

The fact that a speaker accepts a given sentence is the product of two factors – its meaning, and what the speaker believes. Given that we know what the sentence means, we can infer what he believes, and conversely. The problem is that, in radical interpretation, neither can

---

11  *Inquiries into Truth and Interpretation*, 200. See also 168.
12  "The Structure and Content of Truth," 314.
13  For this concept, see esp. essay 9 in *Inquiries*.

be presupposed, which means that the evidence available to a radical interpreter does not discriminate between innumerable ways of ascribing meanings to the speaker's sentences. Given any set of meanings ascribed to the sentences held true, we could make compensating assumptions about what he believes so as to fit the evidence. For example, given that the speaker believes that X is red, the fact that he accepts the sentence "X is red" is explained by the hypothesis that the sentence is true if and only if X is red. Given that he believes that X is blue, it is best explained by the hypothesis that the sentence is true if and only if X is *blue*. And so on.

However, to say that the evidence available to a radical interpreter underdetermines theories of interpretation in this way is just another way of saying that radical interpretation is impossible. And that conflicts with the idea of the social nature of meaning. Part of the *rationale* of the principle of charity is that it permits us to resolve the conflict. For the principle of charity allows us to hold one factor (the belief-factor) constant while determining the other. In other words, the room for ascribing truth conditions is limited, and the evidence gets some real bite. Of course, we may perhaps imagine other constraints, which yield the same result, which in turn means that the argument is incomplete. But if we combine it with the intuitive argument mentioned earlier, we get the desired result.

In any case, as we have seen, the principle of charity entails that, if two persons systematically apply a word to different items, this indicates that they use the word to mean different things, because we otherwise must assume that one of them is systematically in error. Could we therefore appeal to this principle in support of the claim that missionaries and cannibals, priests and utilitarians, and so forth, use "good" or "right" to refer (if at all) to different properties? For example, does it support the claim that the egalitarian Rawls and the libertarian Nozick refer to different properties with "just"? In fact, that is not entirely clear.

For example, someone might object that although Rawls and Nozick disagree over the application of "just" they presumably agree in thinking that *if* a state of affairs is correctly labeled "just," we should bring it about, which is enough to ensure sameness of reference. However, this objection is inconclusive. For Rawls and Nozick disagree also over the application of "should." So, the mere fact that they agree over "If a state is just it should be brought about" is not enough to ensure that they assign the same referent to "just," just as the mere fact that two persons agree over

"The bank is next to the stage" is not enough to ensure that they assign the same referent to "bank" (since "stage" is also ambiguous). Similarly, the fact that two persons agree about *one* of the implications of the fact that an item could correctly be described with a certain word is not sufficient for concluding that they use it to refer to the same property. Presumably, socialists and liberals can all agree that democracy is *in some sense* a matter of equality of political influence. This does not guarantee that they assign the same meaning to the term "democracy."

Still, the fact that two persons apply a term differently does not *by itself* imply that it refers to different properties, not even given Davidson's principle of charity. For, as I have kept stressing, according to the version of the principle to which Davidson, Quine and many others subscribe, attribution of errors may be legitimate if there is some plausible *explanation* of the error.

For example, consider the person applying "red" to blue things. If we have reason to think that his eyes do not function properly due to some factor (intoxication), the pressure toward reinterpreting his "red" diminishes. In the case of more "theoretical" terms (such as ethical ones) there is even wider room for explaining error. Thus, consider "psychopath," and suppose that someone applies it to people whom we regard as nonpsychopaths. Unlike in the case of, say, "red," we typically think we need certain collateral information in order to determine when this term is applicable (e.g., information about past behavior). So if someone applies "psychopath" to a nonpsychopath, one way to explain his error is to conjecture that he lacks the relevant collateral information.

The reason why the existence of such an explanation makes it reasonable to hold on to the idea that he still uses "psychopath" to refer to the same property as we do is that it does not exclude that we, ultimately, agree about what counts as *evidence* for predications of the word in question. Agreement of that kind (about its "criteria of application") may be enough to ensure co-reference, as the crucial question is whether he *would* agree with us under favorable conditions; that is, if he were better placed from a cognitive point of view.

However, if we have reason to think that this counterfactual does *not* hold – if the "criteria of application" he associates with the term differs radically from ours – then we have reason to think that he uses "psychopath" in an idiosyncratic way. This is why the disputes for which the ambiguity condition most plausibly holds are those that are *radical*. For when a dispute over an ethical sentence is radical, then it is not true that the disagreement would go away if the parties were better informed about the relevant evidence, and so forth. Thus, given the principle of charity, such disputes satisfy the ambiguity condition.[14] So, as the assumption that a dispute over an ethical sentence is radical does not exclude that each of the parties feel "the need of refuting his opponent's statement as though this were necessary to support his own," and so on, we have reason to accept the ambiguity claim.

## 5.5. THE CAUSAL THEORY OF REFERENCE

The typical realist response to this reasoning is to reject the views on meaning and reference on which it relies and to argue that, given more plausible views, the facts to which the advocates of the argument appeal do not undermine co-reference.

For example, Richard Boyd and David Brink apply a *causal* theory of reference to ethical terms; that is, a theory of the kind associated with writers such as Kripke and Putnam.[15] Given such a view, roughly, a term refers to the item or property that causally regulates our use of that term (in some appropriate way). Because the fact that two persons apply a term differently, and on different grounds, does not exclude that their use of it is regulated by the same property, such considerations need not undermine co-reference, given a causal view, or so it is held.

However, it is not clear that Boyd's version of the causal theory really does have the sought-for implication. Boyd writes:

*Roughly*, and for nondegenerate cases, a term $t$ refers to a kind (property, relation, etc.) $k$ just in case there exist causal mechanisms whose tendency is to bring it about, over time, that what is predicated of the term $t$ will be approximately true of $k$ (excuse the blurring of the use-mention distinction).[16]

---

14  This is really a bit oversimplified, as it is impossible to be exact about the conditions under which a disagreement, given Davidson's theory, involves a genuine conflict of beliefs. After all, that is what Quine's attack against the analytic/synthetic-distinction is all about. For Quine's attack, see "Two Dogmas of Empiricism," reprinted in *From a Logical Point of View* (2nd ed.). New York: Harper & Row, 1961, 20–46.

15  See Boyd, "How To Be a Moral Realist," and Brink, *Moral Realism*, esp. Chapter 6. Boyd explicitly claims that one of the advantages of combining moral realism with a causal account of reference is that it permits the realist to give the right verdict on the kind of cases to which the argument from ambiguity appeals (186f). For Kripke's and Putnam's views see *Naming and Necessity*. Oxford: Blackwell, 1980, and H. Putnam, "The Meaning of 'Meaning'," in *Mind, Language, and Reality*. Cambridge: Cambridge University Press, 1975, 215–271, respectively.

16  "How to Be a Moral Realist," 195.

As examples of such mechanisms, he mentions procedures that are "accurate for recognizing members or instances of $k$ (at least for easy cases)" as well as "the social transmission of certain relevantly approximately true beliefs regarding $k$, formulated as claims about $t$." The problem is that this seems to imply that, unless a speaker $a$ applies $t$, in general, to things that belong to (or have) $k$, $t$ does not refer to $k$ in $a$'s idiolect. But then radical differences regarding how to apply a term provide a reason to doubt co-reference also given Boyd's theory.

Moreover, and more important, even if Boyd's theory yields a different conclusion for some cases compared with the Davidsonian approach, it does not rule out the possibility of disputes for which the ambiguity condition holds altogether. At best, it allows realists to say that the ambiguity condition holds for other cases than those on which, for example, Hare focuses. Nor does it exclude that those cases may display the features that make it counterintuitive to regard them as merely apparent.

This is stressed by Terrence Horgan, Mark Timmons, and Michael Smith. Horgan and Timmons invite us to imagine a "moral twin earth." The inhabitants of this planet use "right" in much the same way as we do (they tend to perform actions to which they attribute "right," they take similar considerations to be relevant in assessing such attributions, and so forth). However, their use of the term is regulated by a different property. So, Boyd has to conclude that our disputes with the "twin-earthlings" are merely apparent. And this seems wrong, given that they use the term in the same way as we do.[17]

Similarly, Smith imagines that we may come across a community where the word "right" plays the same role in their lives as it plays in ours ("in a practice much like moral practice"), even if their use of the term is regulated by a different property from the one that regulates our use. Given the latter assumption, Boyd's theory implies that our disputes with the aliens over the application of "right" are merely apparent. Given the former, the conclusion is supposed to be counterintuitive.[18]

---

17  They develop this argument in "Copping Out on Moral Twin Earth," *Synthese* 124 (2000), 139–152, "New Wave Moral Realism Meets Moral Twin Earth," *Journal of Philosophical Research* 16 (1990–91), 447–65, "Troubles on Moral Twin Earth," *Synthese* 66 (1992), and "From Moral Realism to Moral Relativism in One Easy Step," *Critica* 28 (1996), 3–39. For a recent critique, see D. Merli, "Return to Moral Twin Earth," *Canadian Journal of Philosophy* 32 (2002), 207–40. See also D. Copp, "Milk, Honey, and the Good Life on Moral Twin Earth," *Synthese* 124 (2000), 113–37.

18  *The Moral Problem*, 32–5.

Are these arguments convincing? Someone might object that the truth of the claim that the aliens use "right" in "much the same way as we do" rules out that their use is regulated by a different property, given a proper understanding of what "regulate" means in Boyd's theory. That this objection is no good is seen once we notice that the arguments merely presuppose that our disputes with the aliens could display the appearance of genuine disagreements mentioned earlier. And that seems fully compatible with the assumption that the aliens' use of "right" is regulated by a different property, more or less regardless of how we fill in the details of Boyd's sketch.

There is a straightforward explanation of why Boyd's causal theory does not permit a realist to avoid the problematic cases. Suppose that someone utters the sentence "The death penalty is just." What is it that determines whether we feel opposed to that person in the relevant way? Hardly facts about what property it is that regulates his use of "just." In "deciding" whether to regard this person as a genuine opponent – that is, whether to listen to his arguments, and to try to convince him by offering arguments of our own, and so on – we simply don't care about which property it is that regulates his use of "just." What we care about, I submit, is whether he is disposed to help maintain institutions he describes with that word and to overthrow those he labels "unjust," and whether the arguments he offers have at least *some* relevance also given our own fundamental moral views. The reason is that it is under those conditions, and those only, that it is possible and worthwhile to convince him. The shared background allows us to find arguments that have at least some likelihood of affecting his judgments.

Those conditions can obtain, however, independently of which property it is that regulates his use of "just." This is why we can imagine disputes over the application of "just" that display the relevant appearance of genuine disagreement, even if the parties' use of the disputed term is regulated by different properties.

## 5.6. SOCIAL EXTERNALISM

Let us consider another attempt to let realists off the ambiguity-hook. The causal theory is externalist. It holds that, in the case of some terms at least, which referents they have in a speaker's idiolect is determined by factors that are external to the speaker. This is why individual differences (for example in use) need not undermine co-reference.

Another externalist theory is Tyler Burge's *social* version.[19] According to this theory, the contents and meanings of (some of) the utterances and thoughts of an individual are determined by certain social facts; facts about *other* members of the community to which the individual belongs, especially those who are more expert than him. To take Burge's famous example, doctors know that arthritis is a condition of the joints only, and apply "arthritis" accordingly. Because it is their use that determines its reference also for other speakers, when someone says "I have arthritis in my thigh," this means that he has a false belief, not that the term in question has a different meaning in his idiolect.

Could this theory help the moral realist to respond to the argument from ambiguity? One obvious problem is how to identify those who should be treated as experts, which seems especially pressing in the moral case. However, the main problem in the present context is that the theory cannot handle disagreements between members of *different* communities. Reconsider Hare's example. Presumably, the missionary and the cannibals belong to different communities. Thus, they are obliged to defer to different experts; whose uses may differ in such a way that "good" refers to different properties in their respective languages. Still, disputes between the missionary and the cannibals over the application of "good" may exhibit the appearance of real conflicts, and it seems wrong to regard them as merely verbal.

Again, there is a straightforward explanation of why this suggestion fails. In considering whether to regard someone as our opponent when he applies "good" to something that we would not describe with that term we do not care about whether he belongs to a different community in Burge's sense. What we care about is merely whether it is possible and worthwhile to change his mind by using arguments. This is why Burge's view does not rule out that disputes over predications of ethical terms may display the relevant appearance of a genuine disagreement even if the parties assign different referents to those terms.[20]

19  See Burge's "Individualism and the Mental," in P. French, T. Uehling, and H. Wettstein (eds.), *Midwest Studies in Philosophy* 4, Minneapolis: University of Minnesota Press, 1979, 73–121 and "Individualism and Psychology," *Philosophical Review* 95 (1986), 3–45.

20  A third version of externalism is Ruth Millikan's "teleosemantics," which is elaborated, for example, in her *Language, Thought and Other Biological Categories*, Cambridge, MA: MIT Press, 1984. However, in my view, at the present stage, this theory is so underdeveloped that it is meaningless to try to determine its implications for the argument from ambiguity. For a discussion of its relevance to moral realism, see W. F. Harms, "Adaptation and Moral Realism," *Biology and Philosophy* 15 (2000), 699–712; and R. Joyce, "Moral Realism and Teleosemantics," *Biology and Philosophy* 16 (2001), 725–34.

A third prominent alternative in current philosophy of language is "conceptual role semantics." Given standard formulations of this approach, it may seem far-fetched to think that it may provide any consolation for the realist in the present context. Ned Block, one of its proponents, conceives of conceptual role as "a matter of the causal role of the expression in reasoning and deliberation and, in general, in the way the expression combines and interacts with other expressions so as to mediate between sensory inputs and behavioral outputs."[21] But even if the acceptance of a sentence that predicates an ethical term often may lead to the same behavioral output, our grounds for such predications differ radically. Given Block's account, this indicates that the expression has different meanings in our respective idiolects.

However, Ralph Wedgwood has recently developed a version of conceptual role semantics that is intended to avoid this implication.[22] Wedgwood suggests that the meaning of a term is given by the "rules of rationality" governing its use. In the case of evaluative expressions (including moral ones), the relevant rules are "rules of practical reasoning." Wedgwood asks what it is for a four-place predicate $B$ to mean the same as the evaluative predicate occurring in the following sentence; "$x$ is (all things considered) a better thing for $z$ to do at $t$ than $y$." In particular, he focuses on sentences that are in first person (where $z$ stands for "me") and regards the present or future. The idea is that "$B(x, y, \text{me}, t)$" means the same as "$x$ is (all things considered) a better thing for me to do at $t$ than $y$" (where $t$ refers to a present or future time) if and only if its use is governed by the following rule:

Acceptance of "$B(x, y, \text{me}, t)$" commits one to having a preference for doing $x$ over doing $y$ at $t$.

Wedgwood argues that this account can be extended to other evaluative and moral expressions, such as "wrong." Moreover, one of its advantages,

---

21  "An Advertisement for a Semantics for Psychology," reprinted in S. Stich and T. Warfield (eds.), *Mental Representation: A Reader*, Oxford: Blackwell, 1994, 93. Further on in the paper, he qualifies this claim: "Conceptual role abstracts away from all causal relations except the ones that mediate inferences, inductive or deductive, decision making, and the like" (94). See also his "Functional Role and Truth Conditions," *Proceedings of the Aristotelian Society*, Supp. Vol. 61 (1987), 157–81, and H. Field, "Logic, Meaning and Conceptual Role," *Journal of Philosophy* 69 (1977), 379–408.

22  See his "Conceptual Role Semantics for Moral Terms," *Philosophical Review* 110 (2001), 1–30.

he thinks, is that it allows a realist to explain why people may be in genuine moral disagreement even if they are rational and share nonmoral beliefs (i.e., even if the dispute is radical). Suppose that one person says that meat eating is wrong while another denies this, and that their dispute is radical. They may still mean the same with "wrong," according to Wedgwood, as they may both "master the rule according to which certain moral beliefs commit one to a certain sort of *preference* or endorsement of *attitude*."[23]

Does Wedgwood's account permit a realist to respond to the argument from ambiguity? One worry is that it may seem more congenial with noncognitivism. However, Wedgwood argues that it can, after all, be reconciled with cognitivism (and thus with realism).

Reconsider B. In arguing that his account can be reconciled with cognitivism, Wedgwood concentrates on trying to show how the relevant rule determines the reference or semantic value of B. Why is this important? The reason seems to depend on his views about the content of cognitivism. Wedgwood takes cognitivism to imply that there is a property such that the meaning of an evaluative expression determines that it stands for that property. Presumably, this entails that, if it is assumed that the meanings of evaluative expressions are given by certain rules of practical reasoning, a cognitivist must explain how their referents are determined by those rules.

More specifically, Wedgwood takes the relevant task to be to show that there is a referent that can be assigned to B such that the truth of "$B(x, y, \text{me}, t)$" makes it necessary that it is correct to prefer $x$ to $y$, and a mistake to prefer $y$ to $x$. What do "correct" and "mistake" mean? This is to be explained in relation to the "goal" of the kind of reasoning one is engaged in. In the case of "theoretical" reasoning, the goal, he suggests, is to avoid holding false beliefs, which means that the relevant notion of a mistake is that of a false belief. However, practical reasoning, which is the relevant form of reasoning here, also has a goal. A preference is "correct," he suggests, if it is permitted by that goal and "incorrect" if it requires that one does not have it.

Wedgwood does not want to specify the goal of practical reasoning. He stresses that there are many different views about this, including Aristotelian, Kantian, and Humean views. But all of them, he thinks, permit one to prefer $x$ over $y$ whenever $x$ is better than $y$, and require that

23   "Conceptual Role Semantics for Moral Terms," 32.

one not prefer $x$ over $y$ whenever $y$ is better than $x$, which is the crucial issue here. He goes on to say that $B$, and the evaluative expression that occurs in the sentence "$x$ is (all things considered) a better thing for $z$ to do at $t$ than $y$" refers to

that four-place relation between $x$, $y$, $z$, and $t$, such that, necessarily, the "goal" of practical reasoning permits an agent $z$ to prefer doing $x$ over doing $y$ at time $t$, and requires that $z$ not prefer doing $y$ over doing $x$ at $t$, if and only if, $x$, $y$, $z$, and $t$ stand in that relation.

However, in my view, Wedgwood's proposal, though interesting and novel, does not help a realist. For example, it might be questioned whether there is *a* "goal" of practical reasoning analogous to the goal of theoretical reasoning, and whether a realist should commit himself to that idea. It also might be questioned whether every candidate really does require that one not prefer $x$ over $y$ whenever $y$ is better than $x$. It seems to me that facts about the relations between an agent's preferences and beliefs may make it reasonable for him to prefer $x$ over $y$ even if $y$ is better, just as such facts (e.g., the possession of misleading evidence) may make it reasonable for him to believe a falsehood.

However, the main problem in the present context is that realism is conceived as a *continuity thesis* (see Section 1.8). It says that moral judgments are beliefs not different in kind from the beliefs of areas such as, say, physics, where this partly means that their contents are determined in the same way.[24] Wedgwood's account, by contrast, entails that their contents are determined differently. The meanings of terms in physics are given by rules of theoretical reasoning, whereas the meanings of moral terms are given by rules of practical reasoning. This is to surrender the game to the antirealist.[25]

The point I have just tried to make can be couched in more general terms. In order to avoid altogether the possibility of cases which satisfy the ambiguity condition, but where the parties "feel opposed" in the relevant way, a realist could always *devise* a theory of reference or meaning that

24  As Sayre-McCord puts it, realism should be "seamless" in that it holds that "whichever theories of meaning and truth are offered for the disputed [moral] claims must be extended as well to apply to all claims" ("The Many Moral Realisms," 6).

25  I am inclined to think that the same holds for a proposal by Richard Miller that is somewhat related to Wedgwood's. Miller argues that radical differences in the use of moral terms need not mean that our disputes over them satisfy the ambiguity condition on the ground that their contents are determined in such a way that they should be useful for certain projects involving practical reasoning (e.g., for "preventing through rational persuasion fights that would be generated by narrow self-interest"). See Miller *Moral Differences*, Chapter 5.

yields the desired result. That is, he could design a theory that takes the feeling of opposition in *itself* as the criterion of co-reference.

The problem with this suggestion is that, unless the realist can show that the theory he may thus come up with has some independent support, such a move appears entirely *ad hoc*. Moreover, the fact that realism is conceived of as a continuity thesis excludes adopting a theory of cognitive content that is supposed to apply *only* to moral discourse. So, by appealing to a particular theory, the realist commits himself to thinking that it applies to other discourses as well; that is, also to our beliefs about physics. And why think that our motivational attitudes toward the items to which we apply "electron" have anything to do with whether we use it to refer to the same kind of items?

There is an even simpler argument against the theory that takes the feeling of opposition as in itself the criterion of co-reference. Everyone agrees that people can believe *falsely* that they assign the same referent to a term whose application they disagree about. Surely, this belief can induce "feelings of opposition" of the relevant kind. Given the present view on reference, however, that would be enough to ensure co-reference. And this conflicts with the assumption from which we departed, namely that the people in question believe falsely that they assign the same referent to the term in question. The upshot is that *no* theory to which a realist can consistently appeal excludes the possibility of disputes over ethical sentences that, on the one hand, satisfy the ambiguity condition, and, on the other hand, display the relevant appearance of a genuine disagreement.

## 5.8. EXPLAINING DISAGREEMENT

So far, I have discussed the plausibility of the ambiguity claim. I shall now turn to its *significance*. Why would the truth of that claim pose a threat to realism? After all, "grass" has different referents in different idiolects and contexts (for farmers and hippies, say). Presumably, this does not refute realism about grass. Why think otherwise in the case of ethical terms?

Many realists concede that if it could be shown that ethical terms refer to different properties for different speakers, realism is in trouble. Thus, Nicholas Sturgeon admits that if this were true, realism would yield implications that go "contrary to deeply held intuition."[26] Similarly, Richard Boyd takes it for granted that realists are committed to the

---

26  Sturgeon, "Moral Disagreement and Moral Relativism," 101.

view that "[t]here is [. . .] a single objective property which we're all talking about when we use the term 'good' in moral contexts."[27] But isn't this to admit too much? Realists must construe disputes over ethical sentences that satisfy the ambiguity condition as being merely apparent. So what? So far, I have assumed that it is the mere counterintuitiveness of this conclusion that provides the problem. However, in my view, mere intuition is a shaky basis for an argument. I shall therefore pursue another approach.

According to one suggestion, the fact that realists must construe some moral disagreements as merely apparent undermines realism since it leaves realists with no way of explaining the *appearance* of a genuine disagreement that those disagreements might still display. However, one may imagine several responses to that suggestion.

For example, suppose that two persons disagree about whether to apply "just" to a certain institution, and that the dispute displays the appearance of a genuine disagreement. Suppose also that they assign different referents to "just." This does not rule out that a realist can explain the appearance of a real disagreement, it might be held, since he can argue that the dispute concerns how to *decide* the extension of "just" in this particular case. Analogously, consider vague terms. Two persons can disagree about whether to apply, say, "boat" to a borderline case, even if they recognize that it lacks (initially, or in ordinary speech) a determinate extension. What they disagree about is how to *stipulate* the extension (for some particular purpose).

Against this response, one may object that a realist has to explain the appearance of disagreement in *realist* terms; that is, in a way that essentially invokes realist assumptions. That is, a realist may appeal to the idea that the dispute is a disagreement about how "just" *should* be defined only if that disagreement in turn can be construed as a conflict of beliefs. And this requirement need not be satisfied. For example, the mere fact that we disagree about whether to apply "should" to the decision to apply "just" to the institution does not ensure that it is met, because "should" also might have different referents in our respective idiolects.

But *why* should we require that realists be able to explain such appearances in realist terms? For example, why can't realists account for the appearance of opposition by assuming that the parties (falsely) *believe* that there is a conflict of beliefs? That strategy may at least cover some cases.

27 "How to Be a Moral Realist," 186.

More importantly, why can't realists *concede* that the best explanation of the appearance assumes that there is a clash of attitudes? After all, the claim that the parties to such disputes have clashing attitudes is not incompatible with realism. Realism implies that moral judgments consist of beliefs. But this does not exclude that ethical sentences are often used to express desires as well, and that clashes of desires in some cases underlie disputes over such sentences.

This is basically the response suggested by Frank Jackson and Philip Pettit in their article "A Problem for Expressivism."[28] Given their construal of the argument from ambiguity, it claims that two persons, *a* and *b*, can disagree over an ethical sentence such as "*x* is right," and still "agree completely about how things are." Realists hold that a moral disagreement is genuine only if the parties *do* disagree over some fact. So, if they disagree over an ethical sentence but agree over all the facts, realists must regard their dispute as merely apparent, which is supposed to be the wrong conclusion.

Jackson and Pettit respond by pointing out that if *a* and *b* agree over all the facts the sense in which they may still be in disagreement, is, presumably, that they have different conative attitudes toward *x*. But the view that *a* and *b* may disagree in *that* sense is not ruled out by realism. Why would realists have to deny that differences in attitude might survive agreement over facts? In other words, realists seem able to agree with expressivists about the correct diagnosis of the dispute.

I shall shortly explain why I think this response is not satisfactory. Before that, however, let me briefly mention another (but related) option. I have stressed that realists are committed to the view that two persons disagree morally only if they have incompatible beliefs. This is why they must construe cases such as the one with *a* and *b* as merely apparent. However, one could drop that view, and instead adopt some form of relativism. This would allow us to think that *a* and *b* are in genuine moral disagreement in spite of the fact that they agree over all the facts. Why? Because relativism implies that a speaker's "right" could be translated with ours even if we use the term to refer to different properties. Given the concept of a moral disagreement suggested in Section 2.3, the fact that his "right"

---

28  Jackson and Pettit call the argument "The Argument from the Persistence of Moral Disagreement." Notice that Jackson's and Pettit's main aim is to question whether the argument provides a reason to prefer expressivism to *subjectivism*, which is a relativist and antirealist form of cognitivism. However, they indicate that the response they develop can be employed also by other forms of cognitivism. In any case, this is the assumption under which I discuss the argument.

could be translated with ours is sufficient for regarding our disputes with him over its application as genuine. Of course, by adopting relativism, we reject realism. However, we may hold on to cognitivism. And cognitivism is usually taken to be the prime target of the argument from ambiguity.[29]

## 5.9. THE GIST OF THE ARGUMENT

Still, I shall argue that none of these responses is satisfactory. In spelling out this argument, I need to rehearse some of the suggestions made in Chapter 1.

Realists are cognitivists, and cognitivists disagree with expressivists about the nature of moral judgments. Cognitivists think that moral judgments consist of beliefs, while expressivists think that they consist in certain conative attitudes (such as desires).[30]

In Chapter 1, I pointed out that there are certain features of our use of a set of sentences and expressions that "make" them ethical, for example their role in decision making. I also argued that cognitivism is justified to the extent that these features are best explained by assuming that someone's sincere utterance of an ethical sentence is a manifestation of the fact that he has a belief. And expressivism, by contrast, is justified to the extent that the best explanation rather invokes the assumption that the utterance manifests a conative attitude. Thus, consider the fact that people who embrace "It is right to give to charity" often have some tendency to act accordingly. This provides some support for expressivism, since the claim that someone's sincere utterance of the sentence represents a desire to give to charity readily explains that tendency.

Some features of our use of ethical sentences are especially thought to support cognitivism. For example, people behave in various ways *as if* disagreements over ethical sentences are disputes over matters of fact. Thus, we engage in debate over ethical sentences, we develop arguments,

29  In so far as a relativist chooses to concede that a dispute that satisfies the ambiguity condition is merely apparent, he too may try to account for the appearance of a genuine conflict that it may still display by appealing to the assumption that the parties falsely believe that it is genuine, at least if he can provide a plausible explanation of why they are in error. This response has recently been suggested by James Ryan in his paper "Moral Relativism and the Argument from Moral Disagreement," *Journal of Social Philosophy* 34 (2003), 377–386.

30  As I noted in Chapter 1, we may also imagine "hybrid" theories, according to which moral judgments, just as intentions and resolutions, consist of mixtures or combinations of beliefs and desires.

respond to objections, and sometimes succeed in persuading others by our argumentation. These features comprise what we, following Michael Smith, may call "the objectivity of moral judgement." The reason why these features provide support for cognitivism is that cognitivism permits us to offer a very straightforward explanation of them. Why do people behave as if moral disagreements are disputes over matters of fact? Because they *are* issues over matters of fact. What could be a better explanation?[31]

Cognitivists are in the position to offer this explanation since they assume that moral judgments are beliefs. This and this *only* is what allows them to construe moral disagreements as conflicts of beliefs. And that in turn is why cognitivism derives support from the objectivity of moral judgment.

The assumption that two persons have incompatible beliefs explains the aspects that comprise the objectivity of moral judgment through rationalizing them. Thus, recognition of the fact that someone holds a belief that is incompatible with one's own prompts us to feel challenged, because only one of the beliefs that are in conflict can be true. And because we are convinced about the truth of our own belief, we want to be able to respond to the challenge. Therefore, we develop arguments. However, because we also have the general aim of obtaining true and avoiding false beliefs, and try to revise our beliefs so as to achieve this aim, we are responsive to counterarguments.

In other words, consider the following case:

 (i) *a* and *b* give different verdicts upon "*x* is wrong."
 (ii) *a* and *b* are disposed to engage each other in discussion, they "feel opposed," they develop arguments and so on.

The assumption that the verdicts of *a* and *b* represent beliefs permits us to see their dispute as a conflict of beliefs. This in turn provides a plausible explanation of the facts referred to by (ii), which is why cognitivism obtains support from cases for which (i) and (ii) hold.

But now it becomes crucial whether the dispute described in (i) *can* be construed as a conflict of beliefs. For if we add . . .

(iii) The dispute satisfies the ambiguity condition.

---

31  For the view that this provides one reason for being a cognitivist, see for example, Stout, *Ethics After Babel*, 17, and Smith, *The Moral Problem*, Chapter 1, and "Objectivity and Moral Realism: On the Significance of the Phenomenology of Moral Experience," in J. Haldane and C. Wright (eds.), *Reality, Representation and Projection*, Oxford: Oxford University Press, 1993, 235–255, 250.

. . . this is not so. In such cases, we must explain the facts mentioned by (ii) in some other way. For instance, we may assume that the parties have clashing conative attitudes toward $x$, or that they falsely believe that they have incompatible beliefs.

Of course, these assumptions are not incompatible with cognitivism, or with the claim that ethical sentences express beliefs. However, they are *external* to cognitivism, and the claim that ethical sentences express beliefs does not *contribute* anything to the explanation. Therefore, cognitivism fails to derive support from some of the relevant evidence. More important, it fails to derive support from the evidence that is supposed to point most strongly in favor of cognitivism. In my view, this is the real gist of the argument from ambiguity.

Someone might respond that cognitivism at least obtains support from the appearance of disagreement in cases that *can* be construed as conflicts of belief. This is so, it might be held, even if there are *other* cases in which cognitivists have to appeal to clashes of desires. However, such a response is unsatisfactory. For, other things being equal, we should prefer a theory that accounts for a set of phenomena in the same way to one that requires two strategies. Accordingly, we may doubt also that cognitivism provides a plausible account of, and thus derives support from, cases that *can* be construed as conflicts of belief.

We can now explain why the responses considered in Section 5.8 are flawed. According to the first response, cognitivists have no reason to deny that ethical sentences, besides expressing beliefs, also express certain pro- and con-attitudes. Accordingly, they have no reason to deny that it is a clash of attitudes that underlies the fact that the parties to a dispute that satisfies the ambiguity condition still "feel opposed." Therefore, such cases provide no reason to prefer expressivism to cognitivism.

This response misses the mark. Why be a cognitivist? One reason is that cognitivism, uniquely, allows us to conceive of moral disagreements as conflicts of beliefs, which provides a plausible explanation of why people who are in moral disagreement behave *as if* moral disagreements are conflicts of beliefs. The argument from ambiguity aims to show that there are independent reasons against thinking that this *is* the best explanation. If true, that claim deprives cognitivism of one crucial advantage. To insist that alternative explanations are compatible with cognitivism does not help. The point is not that cognitivists must account for disputes for which (iii) holds by appealing to assumptions that are *incompatible* with cognitivism. The point is that they must appeal to assumptions that are *external* to cognitivism.

104

There is a different way to state this. In my view, the aim of the argument is not to illustrate that having clashing attitudes is *one* way to be in moral disagreement. Rather its aim is to show that having incompatible beliefs is not *the* way; a claim that is *inferred* rather than simply *assumed* from the start. Let me explain.

What I did in Chapter 1 was to suggest that the notion of a moral judgment is an *explanatory* notion. Given this view, we have reason to believe that moral judgments have the features we must ascribe to them in order for the attributions of moral judgments to explain what we want them to explain. Something similar holds for the derived notion of a moral disagreement (i.e., the notion of a conflict of moral judgments). For example, one advantage of cognitivism is that it allows us to construe moral disagreements as conflicts of beliefs. This is a clear advantage, since, given that view of the nature of moral disagreements, assumptions to the effect that people disagree morally provide plausible explanations of the aspects of our use of ethical sentences that comprise the objectivity of moral judgment.

What the argument from ambiguity aims to do, however, is to challenge the latter claim. More specifically, it points out that there are cases where people manifest the relevant behavior, but where this cannot be explained by assuming that they disagree morally, given that to be in moral disagreement is to have incompatible beliefs. Thus, we should adopt some other view of the nature of moral disagreements, a view that permits us to treat all cases in a unitary way. And this means that cognitivism loses its advantage.

The foregoing remarks also explain why it does not help cognitivists to resort to some form of relativism. To be sure, this means that they can adopt an alternative notion of a moral disagreement (such as the expressivist notion that to be in moral disagreement is to have clashing attitudes, or some "mixed" notion, given which the parties to a moral disagreement sometimes, but not always, involve conflicts of beliefs).[32] And that in turn might allow them to construe all disputes for which (i) and (ii) hold as genuine moral disagreements. However, by committing themselves to an idea about the nature of a moral disagreement that is neither prompted by

32 Which *is* "the expressivist notion" of a moral disagreement? I have assumed that expressivists analyze moral disagreements in terms of clashes of conative attitudes, which is an assumption that needs elaboration. The important point in the present context, however, is that it does not require a conflict of beliefs. Moreover, in my view, as I have defined disagreement in terms of translation, the best way of characterizing it is in terms of constraints on translation manuals.

nor justifiable in terms of the idea that moral judgments consist of beliefs, this would leave them with little reason for remaining cognitivists.[33]

## 5.10. CONCLUDING REMARKS

The success of the argument from ambiguity means that the response to the other versions of the argument from disagreement that I have called "the semantic move" (see, for example, Section 4.10) is blocked. So, the combination of these arguments is a tougher challenge for realism than any of them taken by itself.

But a more important conclusion of the discussions in this chapter has to do with the *explanation* of the success of the argument from ambiguity. What underlies its success is, the fact that the considerations which determine whether people regard themselves as being in genuine moral disagreement with each other differ from those that are relevant when we are to determine whether they disagree about the truth of some proposition. That is, the considerations we take to be relevant when attributing moral convictions to others are not those one should expect given the realist assumption that such convictions consist in beliefs. Is this feature of our attributional practice somehow wrong? Should we revise our practice? In my view, the answer is no, but the crucial question is if one can provide an independent justification for that answer. This is the topic for the next and final chapter of the book.

33  Of course, there are other reasons for being a cognitivist. For example, there are the "Frege-Geach considerations" mentioned in Chapter 1. However, it is not clear that these considerations support claims that go beyond the thesis that ethical sentences (in some contexts, and for some speakers) express beliefs, and, in virtue of this, are truth apt. And an anticognitivist can consistently accept that thesis. Moreover, notice that the main aim of this book to is to explore whether moral disagreement undermines realism. Whether it also undermines relativist forms of cognitivism is an issue of secondary importance. There is one response to the differences in use on which the argument from ambiguity focuses that I haven't discussed, namely the view that terms such as "right" and "wrong" are *vague* rather than ambiguous, and that the disagreements concern borderline cases. However, borderline cases are characterized by *indecisiveness* rather than fierce disagreement. And even if true, this view doesn't help the realist. For, on any view of vagueness, we cannot rationalize why the parties submit arguments and so on in realist terms (in terms of the aim to seek the truth). The reason is there is no (detectable) truth as to whether a term can be applied to a borderline case.

# 6

## *Attributing Moral Judgments*

### 6.1. INTRODUCTION

The point that the thought experiments about the cannibals and "Moral Twin Earth" are meant to illustrate could be made in terms of translation. Suppose that we encounter an unknown group of people in some remote area, and that we initially don't know their language. Under what conditions is it appropriate to translate some of their linguistic expressions with our ethical terms and sentences? According to Richard Hare, the answer does not depend on whether they apply these expressions differently from the way we apply "right," "wrong," and so on. Nor does it depend on whether their attributions of those terms are based on different nonmoral considerations. And, according to Terrence Horgan and Mark Timmons, the same holds for the fact that their use of the expressions in question is causally regulated by other properties than those that regulate our use of "right" and "wrong."

These views about translation pose a threat to moral realism. At least, they pose a threat in so far as they support the claim that we can correctly translate someone's words with our "right," "good," and so on, in spite of the fact that we assign different truth conditions to sentences that predicate them. For that claim is *incompatible* with realism. According to realism, two persons are in genuine moral disagreement only if there is some proposition whose truth they disagree about. And according to the notion of a moral disagreement adopted in Section 2.3, if someone applies, say, "right" differently from us, we disagree genuinely if his "right" can be translated with ours. Given this notion, realism entails that someone's "right" can correctly be translated with ours only if we assign the *same* truth conditions to sentences that predicate it.

This reasoning illustrates how questions about translation are relevant to the debate about moral realism, a claim that I have kept repeating throughout the book. In the present chapter, I shall elaborate it further. In what follows, I develop a number of arguments against moral realism that rely on views about when it is legitimate to translate someone's sentences with our ethical sentences. I shall then show how these views can be independently justified. This concludes my case against realism.

## 6.2. ATTRIBUTIONAL PRINCIPLES

Consider a translation manual that translates (or gives the contents of) some of the terms and sentences of a given idiolect or language with (or by using) our ethical terms and sentences. That is, suppose that it holds for every ethical term $t$ and sentence $s$ of our language that there is a term $t^\star$ or sentence $s^\star$ of the target idiom such that the manual translates $t^\star$ with $t$ and $s^\star$ with $s$.[1] By an attributional principle, I mean a view that imposes constraints on such a manual. An example is the thesis that, unless the speakers of the target language or idiolect have, in general, some tendency to perform the actions to which they apply a term $t^\star$, a manual that translates $t^\star$ with "right" (and sentences that predicate $t^\star$ with sentences that predicate "right") should be rejected.[2]

The question of which constraints of this kind it is reasonable to impose is intimately related to the question of when it is plausible to attribute moral convictions to other persons. Given information about which sentences the speakers of the target language accept and reject, a manual that translates some of their sentences with our ethical sentences gives us knowledge about which actions or states of affairs or persons the speakers judge to be right, just, good, and so on.[3] For example, if a manual translates a sentence $s$ with our sentence "It is morally right to X," and if the

---

1  In what follows, when I speak of a "manual that translates some of the sentences of the target language with our ethical sentences," I presuppose that it satisfies this ("completeness") condition.

2  Obviously, we need to have come pretty far in the process of interpretation in order to be able to apply this constraint. For example, we need to be able to determine when a speaker refers to a given action by a given term. This means that the task of identifying the ethical vocabulary of the language enters at a rather late stage in the process of interpretation. The important point, however, is that we can ascertain that a manual meets the constraint without assuming from the start that the terms translated by our ethical terms are ethical or not.

3  Conversely, I assume that attributing moral judgments presupposes that an accurate manual translates some of their sentences with some of our own ethical sentences. For a similar view, see Brandt, *Hopi Ethics*, 82.

speakers accept $s$, then the manual represents them as judging that X is morally right.

This means that our views about when to attribute moral judgments, and our criteria for translating some of the sentences of a language with our own ethical sentences, are different sides of the same coin. Accordingly, any attributional principle can be stated either in terms of translation or in terms of attribution. Thus, the constraint just mentioned may be stated as follows: we have, *ceteris paribus*, reason to attribute the judgment that it is right to do X to a person only if he has at least some tendency or motivation to perform X.

## 6.3. THE C-CONSTRAINT

Let us consider another example of an attributional principle. Given a realist view, ethics is a discipline on a par with, say, psychology or physics. In the case of those areas, it is reasonable to require that translation manuals preserve cognitive content. That is, if we wonder which term of an alien language (if any) is to be translated with, say, "electron," we look for a term that refers to the same phenomena.[4] Similarly, if we wonder which sentence of the target language (if any) is to be translated with "Electrons are negatively charged," we look for a sentence with the same truth condition.

The suggestion that offers itself, then, is that realists hold a similar view about ethical terms. In other words, let **T** be a manual that translates some of the sentences of an alien language with our ethical sentences. Realists are committed to regarding the following condition as both necessary and (given certain provisos) sufficient in order for **T** to be acceptable:[5]

For every pair [$s$, $s\star$] such that $s\star$ is a sentence of the target language and $s$ is an ethical sentence of our language, and **T** translates $s\star$ with $s$, $s\star$ expresses the same belief (has the same truth conditions) in the target language as $s$ in our language.

Let us call this condition "the C-constraint." That realists are committed to regarding it as necessary is evident from the fact that they assume that every moral disagreement involves a genuine conflict of beliefs. Suppose that a speaker of the target language rejects a sentence that **T** translates

4   It is helpful to focus on a foreign language when stating these constraints, but it is not crucial, as the question of interpretation may arise also in the case of fellow speakers of one's own language. Interpretation "begins at home."

5   The provisos are imposed to ensure that the manual is not flawed in any other respect (the manual translates not only ethical sentences, but every sentence of the target language). However, we may ignore the question of which these provisos might be.

with our sentence "The death penalty should be abolished." If *we* think that the death penalty *should* be abolished **T** represents us as disagreeing with the speaker. However, unless it satisfies the C-constraint this dispute does not represent a conflict of beliefs.[6]

That realists are committed to regarding it as sufficient is equally evident. Moral realism is the view that ethics is continuous with subject matters such as physics or sociology. This means that, from a realist point of view, the primary function of ethical terms and sentences is to track a certain set of facts and properties. So if there are certain words and sentences of another language that are found to track the same facts and properties, this is sufficient for regarding them as the counterparts of our ethical sentences.

However, I shall argue that these implications of realism are false. The C-constraint is neither necessary nor sufficient. The plan of the chapter is as follows. Sections 6.4–6.6 are devoted to the claim that the C-constraint is not necessary, whereas Sections 6.7–6.9 are devoted to the claim that it is not sufficient. In Section 6.10, I provide independent support for the attributional principles on which the arguments developed in those sections rely. In Section 6.11, finally, some concluding remarks are made.

### 6.4. THE LATITUDE IDEA

The claim that the C-constraint is not a necessary condition of adequate translation may be seen as the upshot of the argument from ambiguity. Thus, in Hare's version, the fact that a person systematically applies "good" differently, and on the basis of radically different considerations, does not rule out our correctly translating his "good" with ours. However, they do, according to some views on meaning and reference, rule out the assumption that we assign the same referent to this term, and the same truth conditions to sentences that predicate it. Hence, given these views, Hare's claim conflicts with the idea that the C-constraint is necessary.

Hare's claim is congenial with the latitude idea, an idea whose content I have indicated by contrasting it with Donald Davidson's views on belief attribution. Consider the attribution of beliefs about subject matters other than ethics. For example, consider the attribution of beliefs about *schizophrenia*, about its causes and treatment. Given Davidson's principle of charity, we may legitimately attribute a specific belief to a person

---

6  The idea that realism presupposes absolutism has been questioned, for example by Paul Bloomfield in his "The Rules of 'Goodness': An Essay on Moral Semantics." I discuss his objections in Chapter 1 (note 45).

about schizophrenia, whether or not we share it, only if we also assume that he has many beliefs that we do share (such as the view that having a college degree is not sufficient for being schizophrenic). In other words, suppose that a manual **T** translates a term *t* of the target idiom with our term "schizophrenic." According to Davidson, **T** is acceptable only if the speakers of the target language are, by and large, disposed to apply *t* to people to whom we are disposed to apply "schizophrenic," or at least take similar considerations as relevant in determining its application. The mere fact that **T** entails that the speaker is in error does not, of course, refute it. But then there must be some way of explaining the difference; for example, in terms of some cognitive shortcoming on the part of the speaker. If this is impossible, we should revise the manual.[7]

Philosophers usually assume that there are limits and constraints of this kind also in the moral case. Some of these are intended to preserve a certain structure among the moral concepts. Thus, a manual that represents the speaker as thinking that impermissible actions are always right should be revised. However, we also impose more substantive constraints, constraints that concern which items *are* right, permissible, and so on. For example, if the speakers never apply a term to actions, but only to, say, trees, this is evidence against translating it with "right." More controversially, some philosophers assume that a thought is to be conceived as the ascription of moral rightness to an action only if the thinker, in evaluating that thought, assigns at least some relevance to the consequences of the action for the well being of others. Let us call constraints of this kind "Footian constraints" (as Philippa Foot was early in noting their plausibility).[8]

However, according to the latitude idea, we should require less agreement, and allow for more error and idiosyncratic views in the case of ethics as compared with other subject matters. For the latitude idea permits us to attribute a moral conviction to a person that we do not share, even

---

7   This is really a bit oversimplified, since particular ascriptions of meanings or truth conditions are, in Davidson's framework, to be tested *holistically*, that is, by seeing whether they follow from a theory of interpretation that *as a whole* fits the evidence better than the alternatives. But those complications have no import in the present context.

8   See Foot, *Virtues and Vices*, Chapters 7 & 8. But see also Smith, *The Moral Problem*, 40ff, and Boyd, "How To Be a Moral Realist," 210ff. Foot, Smith and Boyd are realists. However, many antirealists have expressed similar views. See, for example, Blackburn, "The Flight to Reality," in R. Hursthouse, G. Lawrence, and W. Quinn (eds.), *Virtues and Reasons*. Oxford: Clarendon Press, 1995, 35–75. Moreover, Gibbard insists, in a Footian spirit, that we, in attributing moral judgments to a person, beyond logic, must impute "some substantive moral banalities" (*Wise Choices*, 200).

in the absence of a background of substantial agreement, and even if his verdict cannot be explained away with reference to some (independently specifiable) cognitive fault.

## 6.5. THE LATITUDE IDEA AND MORAL DISCOURSE

One should distinguish between two ways of interpreting the latitude idea. Under the first interpretation, it says that we *do* allow for the latitude in question. Under the second, it says that it is *legitimate* to allow for such latitude. I believe that both these claims are true.[9] However, it is the latter claim that is a premise in the arguments that I develop below, and it is really for this claim that the phrase "the latitude idea" is reserved. In Section 6.10, I shall try to show that the latitude idea can be independently justified. Part of its appeal, however, is that it, either by itself, or as people implicitly accept it, contributes to the explanation of a number of considerations around which current meta-ethical debate revolves.

For example, the latitude idea helps to explain why we may find so much moral diversity in the world, and why, in many cases, the diversity runs so deep compared with other areas. For, given the latitude idea, a wide variety of views, even those that are quite alien to us, are acknowledged as moral. Simply put, the weaker conditions we impose for something to count as an *X*, the more *X*s we'll find.

Moreover, it is this fact that explains why we may find ourselves in disagreements where the hope of a rational resolution seems so remote. It is plausible to assume that in order to achieve such a resolution there must be a "common ground"; that is, a set of shared assumptions that may function as premises in arguments that are recognized as relevant by all parties. Trying to produce a convincing argument in the *absence* of such a background is like trying to win a game without rules. And the tolerance prescribed by the latitude idea permits us to find ourselves in genuine moral disagreement also with those with whom we share no such common ground.[10]

---

9 Of course, there is a question of who the "we" refers to, when I say that "we allow for latitude." However, because the "descriptive" version does not function as a premise in any of my arguments, there is really no need to very exact. Let me also add that I think that something similar to the latitude idea also holds for other areas, such as aesthetics and, in my view, much of philosophy.

10 For the claim that rational persuasion presupposes such "common ground," see P. Davson-Galle, "Arguing, Arguments, and Deep Disagreements," *Journal of Informal Logic* 14 (1992), 147–156.

In effect, the latitude idea is congenial with the claim that ethical concepts are "essentially contestable."[11] To say that ethical concepts are "essentially contestable" is usually taken to mean that although questions about their application (moral issues) *allow* for rational discussion, there is no way to *settle* these debates by rational discussion. The first feature is explained by the fact that we require agreement *at all* (remember the Footian constraints). For these constraints ensure *some* amount of background agreement. The second feature is explained by the latitude idea, because (again) it permits us to find that we disagree with people where the common ground is too slim to enable us to resolve our disputes.

The latitude idea is also congenial with other aspects of moral discourse, such as Hume's law and G. E. Moore's well-known "open question argument." As we know, Moore tried to refute the idea that ethical terms, such as "right," could be defined in terms of some phrase that refers to a natural property. His argument consists in the observation that, for any such property, we may learn that an action has that property and still meaningfully ask whether it is right. What this means is that, for any theory about which natural property it is that makes an action right, we are willing to regard ourselves as being in genuine disagreement with someone who denies that view, which is a conclusion that accords with the latitude idea.

Similarly, consider the claim that if an action has some nonmoral property $P$ then it is morally right. Given this claim, the fact that an action has $P$ implies that it is morally right (at least if we assume that logical relations can hold between moral judgments). According to one construal of Hume's law, it denies that any such "bridge principle" is conceptually or logically true, and entails, as Nicholas Sturgeon puts it, that

even if we have all the nonmoral facts right, and reason in accord with whatever a priori constraints may apply, there is still room for error when we go on to draw moral conclusions.[12]

---

11  The notion of essential contestedness was first introduced by W. B. Gallie. See his "Essentially Contested Concepts," *Proceedings of the Aristotelian Society* 56, (1955–1956), 167–198 and *Philosophy and Historical Understanding*, London: Chatto and Windus, 1964, esp. Ch. 8. That moral concepts are essentially contested is quite commonly held. See, for example S. Hurley, *Natural Reasons*, Oxford: Oxford University Press, 1989, 46–47. Moreover, in "Toward *Fin de Siècle* Ethics," Darwall et al. suggest that antirealism provides a possible explanation of the essential contestedness (see 147).

12  Sturgeon, "What Difference Does It Make Whether Or Not Moral Realism is True?," 128. But see also Brink, *Moral Realism*, 166. See Håkan Salwén's *Hume's Law*, Stockholm: Almqvist and Wiksell, 2003, for a survey of different interpretations of the law.

And this is exactly the kind of conclusion that the latitude idea allows for.[13]

## 6.6. THE LATITUDE IDEA AND THE C-CONSTRAINT

In this section, I shall argue that the latitude idea entails that the C-constraint is not a necessary condition of an adequate translation manual, at least if we combine it with certain Footian constraints. I shall pursue this discussion under the assumption that ethical sentences do express beliefs. It cannot be unfair against realists to make this assumption.

What does it take in order for the C-constraint to be satisfied? Different theories of cognitive content and reference answer this question differently, which means that they may have different implications for the thesis that the latitude idea entails that the C-constraint is not necessary. That the Davidsonian approach that I have contrasted the latitude idea with lends support for such a conclusion is obvious. Suppose that a manual **T** represents the speakers of the target language as thinking that an action is wrong, even though we think that it is right. The claim that the C-constraint is necessary entails, together with Davidson's views on cognitive content, that **T** is correct only if the verdict it attributes to the speaker is explicable in terms of some cognitive deficiency on behalf of the speaker, and only if it also represents the speaker as, by and large, agreeing with us about the considerations that are relevant in determining whether an action is right. The latitude idea, on the other hand, entails that it could be correct even if these conditions are not satisfied. Thus, it entails that a translation manual need not preserve sameness of cognitive content, given Davidson's view on meaning and reference.

In the case of other theories, the argument has to be different. The arguments that show why the theories surveyed in Chapter 5 have the same implication are essentially the same as those that show that they leave room for the ambiguity claim (see Sections 5.5 through 5.7). There is no real point in repeating these arguments here, and I shall restrict myself to reconsidering the casual theory of reference and in particular Richard Boyd's version.

---

13 The latitude idea is also related to Michael Smith's idea that attempts to provide reductive definitions of normative terms face what he calls "a permutation problem." See *The Moral Problem*, Chapter 2. Notice that I do not want to preclude that there may be alternative explanations to the considerations mentioned in this section.

114

According to Boyd, ethical terms refer to the properties that causally regulate our use of these terms (in the relevant way). So if the same property regulates different speakers' use of "right" it has the same referent for all of them, regardless of whether they use it differently. However, as I argued in Chapter 5, given the details of Boyd's account of what it means to say that someone's use is regulated in the relevant way, it is doubtful whether it does allow for co-reference in the presence of substantial disagreement. Boyd thinks that if a property $k$ regulates a speaker's use of a term $t$ in the relevant sense then there are causal mechanisms whose tendency is to bring it about, over time, that "what is predicated of the term $t$ will be approximately true of $k$,"[14] such as, for example, procedures that are "accurate for recognizing members or instances of $k$." This in turn indicates that, unless a speaker $a$ applies $t$, in general, to things that belong to (or have) $k$, $t$ does not refer to $k$ in $a$'s idiolect. It follows that radical differences regarding how to apply a term undermine co-reference also given Boyd's theory. The latitude idea, however, does *not* rule out our translating $a$'s "right" with ours under those conditions. Hence, the latitude idea entails that the C-constraint is not necessary, even if we accept Boyd's theory.

Again, maybe one *could* somehow cook up an account of what it means for a property to causally regulate someone's use of a term that *does* allow for the possibility that the same property regulates the use of two different persons, even if they disagree widely about its application. However, such a proposal faces other problems.

Thus, it might be suspected that it proves too much. Remember that realists are committed to the idea that the C-constraint is both necessary *and* sufficient. Now, if there are almost no differences in application that are supposed to exclude that the same property regulates different speakers' use of a word, some of the Footian constraints it is reasonable to impose seem entirely unjustified. For example, consider Michael Smith's suggestion that a word of an alien language is to be translated with "morally right" only if its speakers assign at least some relevance to the consequences of the actions on which they apply the word for the well being of other affected individuals. On the version of the casual theory we are now considering, it seems perfectly possible that the C-constraint could be satisfied even if Smith's constraint is not. So, if Smith's constraint is necessary, as I shall argue later, the present version of the causal theory does not yield a plausible version of realism.

---

14  "How to Be a Moral Realist," 195.

The Footian constraint just mentioned may be used in other arguments for the claim that the C-constraint is not necessary, given the causal theory of reference. Below, I shall argue that the constraint in question is not only necessary, but, together with similar constraints (that ensure a certain minimal amount of background agreement), *sufficient* for adequate translation. At least, they are sufficient if we assume that the manual satisfies a further constraint, namely the condition mentioned in Section 6.2. This constraint is met only if the manual represents the speakers of the target language as having at least some motivation to perform the actions they judge to be obligatory and right, and at least some tendency to abstain from actions they judge to be wrong. Thus, if it translates a term of the target language with "obligatory," speakers of the language have some tendency to perform the actions to which they apply that term. Let us call this further constraint "The M-constraint."

If these constraints are sufficient, the C-constraint is not necessary, given the causal theory of reference. Suppose that a manual **T** translates a term *t* with "morally right." Given *any* view of what it means for a property to regulate someone's use of a term, the M-constraint and the Footian constraints just indicated could be satisfied by **T** even if the property that regulates the speakers' use of *t* is different from the one that regulates our use of "morally right." Notice that *any* view to the effect that legitimate translation of ethical terms is determined by something *else* than "joint regulation" permits us to reach the same conclusion.

There is always, of course, the option to *design* a theory of cognitive content that yields the desired result; that is, that allows for the pertinent latitude, and that takes the relevant Footian constraint into proper consideration. But as I have argued earlier (Section 5.7) the plausibility of this move is undermined by the fact that realism is conceived of as a continuity thesis. By relying on a particular theory of cognitive content, a realist commits himself to applying it to all the other discourses he wants to be a realist about. Hence, in order for such a move to be successful he must construct a theory that satisfies the following conditions: (1) it can be *independently* justified as a *general* account of cognitive content; (2) it entails that the kind of differences in use on which the latitude idea focuses do not exclude co-reference, and; (3) it entails that a translation manual is incorrect unless it satisfies the relevant Footian constraints as well as the M-constraint. No such theory has, to my knowledge, been produced.

Let us turn to the thesis that the C-constraint is not sufficient. My argument for this claim invokes the M-constraint. The underlying idea of the M-constraint is the commonly acknowledged fact that people in general have at least some tendency to act in accordance with their moral convictions. Every party of the meta-ethical debate recognizes this fact, although they disagree about the extent to which it allows for exceptions, about its modal scope, and about how the correlation is to be explained. For example, internalists hold that it is best explained by the idea that there is a *necessary* connection between having a moral judgment and being motivated to act in accordance with it, while externalists deny this.

Again, let **T** be a translation manual that translates some of the sentences of the target language with our ethical sentences. **T** satisfies the M-constraint only if the following holds:

If **T** translates a sentence $s\star$ of the target language with "It is morally right to X," and if speakers were to accept $s\star$, then they would (in general) have some tendency or motivation to perform X.

Similar conditions are supposed to hold for the rest of our moral sentences. Thus, if **T** translates $s\star$ with "It is wrong to X," then the speakers have some motivation not to perform X whenever they embrace $s\star$. And so forth. In what follows, I shall argue that the C-constraint is not sufficient, on the ground that a manual can meet the C-constraint and still fail to meet the M-constraint. Because the M-constraint is necessary, the C-constraint is not sufficient.

## 6.8. A THOUGHT EXPERIMENT

Whether a manual can satisfy the C-constraint and fail to satisfy the M-constraint might seem to depend on how the latter constraint should be construed, more specifically. Should we require that *all* speakers of the language are *always* motivated to act in accordance with what they, given the manual, think is just and right, or merely that most of them are motivated most of the time?[15] Or should we perhaps require just that people are motivated insofar as they are rational?[16]

---

15  For example, Blackburn seems to think that his version of internalism allows for the existence of an occasional amoralist (*Ruling Passions*, 61).

16  This way of construing the constraint is congenial with Michael Smith's version of internalism. See *The Moral Problem*, Chapter 5.

How we answer these questions has little import for the argument that I shall develop, however. Its point of departure is the following simple thought experiment. Suppose that the terms $t$ and $u$ of the target language are applied by its speakers to the same actions as those to which we apply "morally right" and "morally wrong," respectively. Suppose also that they take similar considerations to be relevant in determining the extension of $t$ and $u$ as those we take to be relevant in determining the extentions of "morally right" and "morally wrong," and, moreover, that their use of $t$ and $u$ is causally regulated (in the appropriate sense) by the same properties as those that regulate our use of "morally right" and "morally wrong." Indeed, suppose that the speakers' use of $t$ and $u$ has *whatever* features that are sufficient (given any plausible view on meaning and reference to which a realist can consistently appeal) for concluding that if sentences predicating "morally right" and "morally wrong" express beliefs in *our* language, sentences predicating $t$ and $u$ express the same beliefs in theirs.

This assumption is intended to ensure that a manual **T** that translates $t$ with "morally right" and $u$ with "morally wrong" satisfies the C-constraint.[17] However, it does not ensure that it satisfies the M-constraint. For it does not ensure that they are motivated to perform the actions to which they apply $t$ and motivated to abstain from actions to which they apply $u$.

To see this, consider *why* their use of the $t$ and $u$ might have the features that ensure that **T** satisfies the C-constraint. A perfectly possible explanation is that they have developed the vocabulary in question in order to *mimic* our ethical vocabulary. That is, they have consciously developed a vocabulary by which they want to track the same properties as those (if any) that we track with our ethical vocabulary. Why would they want that? Perhaps since they have noted that we assign importance to the question of whether "morally wrong" could be applied to an action, and as the vocabulary helps them to predict our behavior in certain ways, and to conveniently communicate about it.

Analogously, consider teenagers and their parents. In the idiolect of teenagers, "cool" functions in many ways as an evaluative term, and one way for the parents to improve their knowledge of the reactions and

---

17  We assume for example that the speaker's use of $t$, $u$, and so on, displays the same "inferential structure" as our use of "morally right," and "morally wrong," and so on. Thus, they are disposed to reject a sentence that predicate $t$ of a given action if they accept a sentence predicating $u$ about the same action.

behavior of their teenagers is to learn how to use "cool" in accordance with the way it is used by the teenagers. The parents can then use the term to communicate with their children, and among themselves, in a convenient way. "Which pair of jeans should we buy? Let's take those. They are more expensive, but the other pair is less cool. She'll never use them."[18]

Surely, however, the parents could learn this without adopting their children's pro-attitudes toward the things they describe with "cool." My contention is that the same holds in the ethical case. This explains why there may be a set of terms and sentences of the target language such that the use of these terms and sentences exhibit features that ensure that a manual that translates them with our ethical terms satisfies the C-constraint, even if it does not satisfy the M-constraint.[19]

Someone might object that, unless the parents, by and large, share their teenagers' pro- and con-attitudes towards clothes, they *cannot* learn what the items to which they attribute "cool" have in common, and thus cannot learn when it is correct to apply the term. It would be like learning how to use "funny" without having a sense of humor. However, this seems just false. We judge an action to be morally right or wrong on the basis of its natural properties. As long as we apply these terms in a consistent way (which is necessary in order for them to have referents at all) there *is* some natural property that the things we apply them to share. And if there is such a property, there is no reason to think that someone cannot find out *what* it is, regardless of his motivational patterns.[20]

Let us suppose, then, that a manual that translates some of the terms of the target language by our ethical terms could satisfy the C-constraint and fail to satisfy the M-constraint. Given this claim, we may elaborate on the example to provide further support for the claim that the C-constraint is not sufficient. Thus, suppose that, besides the vocabulary that comprises

---

18  Similarly, consider servants who learn to apply "delicious" like their masters in order to become more efficient in satisfying their needs.

19  Blackburn suggests a similar thought experiment in his "Flight to Reality," 48. See also Gibbard, *Thinking How to Live*, 154ff.

20  The argument offered here presupposes that different agents may have significantly different ultimate ("intrinsic") desires. Someone might point out that, according to the Davidsonian approach to which I otherwise have been sympathetic, significant differences in desires are just as inconceivable as massive differences in belief. After all, Davidson emphasizes that a competent interpreter represents an agent as "a believer of truths, and a lover of the good." However, in "Are We Lovers of the Good?" (*Synthese* 138 [2004], 247–260), I argue that Davidson's ideas allow, *pace* what Davidson holds himself, for the fact that there is an asymmetry in this respect between beliefs and desires.

the terms $t$, $u$, and so on, there is another set of terms of the target language ($t^\star$, $u^\star$, etc.). And suppose that a manual $\mathbf{T}^\star$ that translates *these* terms with our ethical terms *does* satisfy the M-constraint, but fails to satisfy the C-constraint.

Again, this illustrates that the C-constraint is not sufficient. For the claim that it is yields the conclusion that $\mathbf{T}$ is preferable to $\mathbf{T}^\star$. And this is the wrong conclusion, at least if we assume that $\mathbf{T}^\star$ satisfies some appropriate set of Footian constraints. If $\mathbf{T}$ is correct, we are led to conclude that the speakers of the target language agree with us about what is right and wrong, and so forth, but that they have no tendency to act accordingly. By contrast, if $\mathbf{T}^\star$ is correct, we are led to believe that they disagree with us (within the limits set by the Footian constraints) about what is right and wrong, but that they do have a tendency to act in accordance with their moral judgments. In effect, we are led to conclude that their moral judgments play the same role for them as our judgments for us. As I shall argue below, this is enough to show that $\mathbf{T}^\star$ is preferable to $\mathbf{T}$.[21] Notice that the story would have been entirely different if we instead were to look for terms translatable with terms such as "red" or "sweet." Then we would look for terms that are applied, by and large, to those things we think are red or sweet. Herein lies, in my view, the key to the best understanding of moral thinking.

### 6.9. REALISM AND THE M-CONSTRAINT

Could a realist respond to the argument set forth in the previous section? For example, could he show that if a manual satisfies the C-constraint, it automatically satisfies the M-constraint as well? This would not only permit him to respond to the argument. It also would allow him to account for the intuitions that fuel internalism.

Any attempt to show that, if a manual satisfies the C-constraint, it satisfies the M-constraint as well, will have to rely both on general views about belief attribution, and on specific views about the contents of the beliefs that are held to constitute our moral judgments (about the nature of the properties we are supposed to attribute by judging actions to be right and wrong, etc.). Let us start with a recent suggestion by Ronald

---

21 The underlying idea of this argument is that cognitivism is implausible since it allows for a community of amoralists. Similar arguments are developed by Blackburn in "The Flight to Reality," 48, and by James Lenman in "The Externalist and the Amoralist," *Philosophia* 27 (1999), 441–457.

Dworkin, who is sympathetic toward a Davidsonian approach. Dworkin writes:

We ascribe beliefs to people as part of a complex process in which we also ascribe motives and meanings so that all three fit together in a way that makes best sense of their behavior as a whole. Given what we take judgments about wrongful conduct to mean, we therefore withhold their attribution unless we find it plausible to suppose that the agent would be moved to some degree to avoid the act he deems wrongful quite independently of other motives he might have for avoiding it, at least absent circumstances that show weakness of the will or emotional disorder. There is nothing queer or bizarre about that attributional strategy.[22]

That is, according to Dworkin, given a plausible account of the *content* of the belief that is supposed to constitute the conviction that it is wrong to perform some action, unless we have reason to think that someone has a tendency not to perform it, we have no reason to attribute that belief to him. This squares with the M-constraint.

But *what* view about the content of that belief would yield such a conclusion? On one suggestion, the content is such that it is *irrational* to have the belief without having a corresponding motivation. Because we do not make "best sense" of a speaker's behavior by attributing beliefs that make him irrational, this allows us to conclude that we should, normally, avoid attributing moral judgments unless there is a tendency to act accordingly.

Let us consider a particular version of this reasoning. Thus, consider the theory proposed by Michael Smith. According to Smith, to think that one should keep a promise is to believe that one *would* desire keeping it if one had a maximally informed, coherent and unified desire set. This belief coheres badly, Smith thinks, with the desire not to keep the promise. After all, in a sense, to desire to do something, and to believe that one would not have that desire if one were fully rational, is to be irrational according to one's own standards. So, given Smith's theory, because we should not attribute beliefs that render a person irrational, we should not, normally, attribute moral judgements in the absence of a corresponding motivation.[23]

But this argument is too swift. Let us concede that a person's system is incoherent if he desires something that conflicts with what he believes he would desire if he had a maximally informed, coherent and unified

---

22  "Objectivity and Truth," 116. See also "Reply to Critics," BEARS, J. Dreier and D. Estlund (eds.), http://www.brown.edu/Departments/ Philosophy/bears/homepage.html.

23  See *The Moral Problem*, esp. Chapter 5.

desire set. That is, suppose that he, in those circumstances, would desire *p*, but that he, as a matter of fact, actually desires not-*p*. It still does not follow that a person, in order for his system to be coherent, must desire everything he thinks he would desire under those circumstances. To desire something that conflicts with what one believes that one would desire under those conditions is one thing. Failing to desire something that one believes one would desire is another. And it is the latter combination that Smith needs to show is irrational in order to substantiate the claim that it is irrational to have moral judgments without being motivated to act accordingly.

Moreover, and more important, it might be questioned whether the kind of incoherence that Smith talks about is a form of irrationality in the *relevant* sense. After all, the beliefs of a person who suffers from such an incoherence may be perfectly consistent with each other, and even be interrelated by, say, explanatory relations in the way, for example, coherentists stress is sufficient for epistemic justification. Moreover, this kind of incoherence is compatible with the possibility that all his current preferences are jointly satisfiable, and that they meet the usual ordering conditions (such as transitivity). It is not clear that there is some notion of incoherence of desires that goes beyond this. In particular, it is not clear that the fact that a manual renders a speaker incoherent in this sense provides a reason to reject it.[24]

Let us consider a more straightforward suggestion. It might be argued that there are evolutionary reasons for thinking that all psychologically normal humans share certain motivational patterns. For example, we are disposed to avoid dangers, and to seek pleasure. Moreover, given the crucial role of cooperation and coordination for the prospects of survival, we all share certain tendencies that are important in promoting those things. This includes a tendency to care for the well-being of others (not only for close kin), to keep promises, and to avoid violent conflict and so on.

Now, consider the term "poisonous." In the case of this term, people are usually realists – they think that "poisonous" refers to a natural property. Still, the motivational patterns shared by all normal humans are such that, if we find that someone believes that a certain mushroom is poisonous, we usually expect him to avoid eating it, if there is no particular reason for thinking that he is atypical. Conversely, if we find that he does

---

24 For the constraints Davidson imposes on the attribution of desires, see in particular "A New Basis for Decision Theory," *Theory and Decision* 18 (1985), 87–98.

*not* have a tendency to avoid eating it, we would hesitate to attribute to him the belief that it is poisonous.

Maybe something similar could be said in the moral case. Thus, it might be argued that, given the motivational patterns shared by normal humans, and given a plausible account of the factual property we ascribe to an action by judging it to be wrong, we legitimately expect that if a person recognizes that an action has this property, he is likely to avoid it. Conversely, finding that he lacks such a tendency provides evidence against attributing to him the belief that it has that property. Accordingly, it might be argued that if a manual satisfies the C-constraint, it satisfies the M-constraint as well.

This is basically the strategy adopted by Richard Boyd. According to Boyd, roughly, an action has the property of being wrong to the extent that it "frustrates vital human needs." And, because Mother Nature has endowed us with a tendency to promote such needs, believing that an action has the property Boyd thinks we ascribe to an action by judging it to be wrong yields, normally, a tendency to avoid it. This permits a realist to accommodate the intuitions that support internalism.[25]

One may imagine a number of variations on this theme. But I think all of them fail. Of course, there may be reason to think that we will never expect to encounter a community where there is no tendency to avoid some of the actions we think wrong (e.g., murder for fun). There is surely much overlap in our motivational patterns. However, anthropologists have gathered enough evidence to show that there exist, or have existed, communities whose ways and motivational patterns differ substantially from ours.[26] This is enough to show that a manual could meet the C-constraint and fail to meet the M-constraint. At least, it shows this if we assume that, in order for a manual to satisfy the C-constraint, all it

---

25  "How to Be a Moral Realist," 215. Boyd indicates that he also has a more ambitious argument. According to this argument, a person who accepts a given moral view, but lacks the relevant motivation, is not only atypical, but subject to a *cognitive* deficiency. This argument is supposed to make realists better placed when it comes to explaining the relationship between evaluating and being motivated. However, I shall not treat the argument separately.

26  An intriguing example is the Ik, a tribe of hunters and gatherers who used to live in the desolate outcroppings of the Kenya/Uganda/Sudan border region. The members of this tribe developed an extreme individualism, possibly because of the very harsh conditions they were forced to live under during a period. This led them to take no consideration of the interests even of close kin (such as children and parents), which is, of course, highly unusual (especially for a tribal society). See Turnbull, *The Mountain People*, New York: Simon & Schuster, 1972, for a vivid exposition of this case. See also my "Are We Lovers of the Good?" for further discussion of theoretical issues regarding the diversity of desires.

takes is that the terms it treats as the counterparts of "right," "wrong," and so on, are applied by the speakers of the language to the same things as those we describe with those words.

Moreover, there is an explanation of why Mother Nature has allowed for this diversity. To be sure, it is crucial for the survival of a community and its members that the motivations of the members exhibit *some* patterns that permit them to resolve conflicts of interests, and to avoid various coordination problems. But these aims can be achieved in more ways than one, and by more than one set of motivational patterns. So the fact that the members of a community are not motivated to avoid (all) the actions we judge to be wrong, or to perform (all) the actions we judge to be right, does not mean that their society will perish. This is why the limits set by Mother Nature allow for the possibility that a manual that translates someone's sentences with our ethical sentence may satisfy the C-constraint even if it fails to satisfy the M-constraint.

## 6.10. EXPLAINING COORDINATION

On the basis of the M-constraint, the latitude idea, and the vaguely indicated set of constraints that I have called "Footian constraints," I have argued that the C-constraint is neither necessary nor sufficient for adequate translation. However, this provides a reason to reject realism only if we have independent reasons to accept those principles. For example, why should a realist, who is usually an externalist, accept the M-constraint? To provide an independent justification is the aim of the present section. This is where the reference to folk psychology, made in Chapter 1, finally does some work.

The only reason there might be for positing moral judgments as a distinct class of states within the context of folk psychology is that it has a distinct role in the explanation of human behavior. Remember the analogy with religions that I made in the Preface. Contemporary anthropologists have a broader conception of a religion than that of many earlier ones. For example, the idea of an omnipotent creator is not seen as an essential element. The reason is that contemporary anthropology associates a certain explanatory role with religions, and in order for a system of convictions to have that role it need not contain that idea.

I shall try to indicate that the states picked out by the latitude idea, in combination with the M-constraint and the Footian constraints, also have a distinct explanatory role or function. The point of departure is a well-known idea: the states that these principles pick out have a crucial role in the explanation of why people manage to coordinate their actions in response to certain types of collective action problems.[27]

The cases I am thinking of are sometimes called "social dilemmas."[28] Social dilemmas occur whenever two or more individuals in interdependent situations have to make independent choices in which the maximization of private goals yields outcomes leaving all worse off (in terms of those goals) than feasible alternatives. For example, suppose that the agents want to maximize their self-interest. These are cases for which it holds that if each rather than none of the members of some group does what will be better for himself, this is worse for everyone. The best-known example is the prisoners' dilemma, in which two agents who have jointly committed a crime have to choose between confessing or not. Given that each wants to minimize his time in prison, and given that their decisions are independent, it is rational for each to confess, even if they thereby achieve an outcome that renders both longer sentences than if both had remained silent.

Social dilemmas occur all over the world and causes and have caused immense suffering. Many such dilemmas involve public goods, such as fisheries, water reservoirs, and so on. Everyone is worse off if the good is not provided or underprovided. Still, it might be rational for each not to contribute, regardless of what the others do. As a consequence, the fisheries, water reservoirs, and so on, are destroyed.

Still, it is a striking fact that agents often manage to dissolve the dilemma, and to coordinate their actions in ways that yield a preferable outcome. How is this possible? The thing to note is that this happens to an extent that cannot be predicted on the basis of the theory that is most dominant in contemporary social sciences, namely rational choice theory. Rational choice theory models humans as self-interested maximizers. However, on this assumption, it is difficult to explain why people

---

27   The reasoning that is developed in what follows is inspired by, and related to, both some of Gibbard's suggestions in *Wise Choices, Apt Feelings*, as well as to some of John Mackie's remarks about "morality in the narrow sense" (see *Ethics*, Chapter 5). It is also related to Richard Miller's discussion in Chapter 5 of *Moral Differences*, and the case he tries to make for his "mixed verdict." However, although we agree about that we should allow for considerable latitude in attributing moral convictions, we do seem to disagree over whether this is compatible with requiring sameness of cognitive content.

28   However, they are called by many names, including "the free-rider problem" (see J. Edney, "Freeriders en Route to Disaster," *Psychology Today* 13 [1979], 80–112), "the tragedy of the commons" (G. Hardin, "The Tragedy of the Commons," *Science* 162 [1968], 1243–1248), and "many-person dilemmas" or "each-we dilemmas" (Parfit, *Reasons and Persons*, Oxford: Oxford University Press, 1984, 59ff).

are disposed to contribute to public goods and to cooperate to the extent that they have been shown to be.[29]

In response to this apparent conflict between theory and evidence one could react in different ways. One response is to adopt a very broad concept of self-interest, and insist, perhaps, that the mere fact that someone *wants* to achieve something shows that the achievement of this goal is what benefits him most. Another is to assume that agents have to take into account various types of uncertainties (regarding, for instance, the possibility that some of those with whom they interact are irrational, or regarding the duration of the situation). However, although these moves might make the theory compatible with the evidence, they also tend to drain it of empirical content. It is no longer clear *what* it predicts. Or better, it predict everything. If you introduce these uncertainties, the number of possible equilibria explodes.[30]

Many social scientists have therefore abandoned the conception of humans as purely self-interested, and assume that the pursuit of self-interest is often constrained by other motivations, motivations that allow them to solve or dissolve their dilemmas. Typical examples are a concern for others, a concern for fairness, and a disposition to keep agreements and to hold promises, even if this yields a sub-optimal outcome in terms of self-interest.[31] For example, if the agents in the prisoners' dilemma had promised each other not to confess, and if they hade been disposed to keep their promises, this would have rendered both less time in prison. In many cases, the presence of such constraints helps to explain why groups manage to avoid problems they would otherwise cause.

The inshore fishery at Alanya, Turkey provides an interesting example. In the early 1970s, unrestrained use of this fishery led to violent conflicts among the users, and to an overwhelming risk of destruction of the common resource. In response to this threat, the anglers devised, with no help from any external agent, a set of rules and institutions for allotting fishing sites. The system prevented both overcapitalization and conflicts over the

29  For a survey of some of the relevant empirical research, see Elinor Ostrom's "A Behavioral Approach to the Rational Choice Theory of Collective Action," *American Political Science Review* 92 (1998), 1–22.

30  Thus, given these forms of uncertainty, there is an extreme increase in the number of possible equilibria. See D. Abreau, "On the Theory of Infinitely Repeated Games with Discounting," *Econometrica* 56 (1988), 383–396.

31  Notice that nothing really hinges on whether these motives do not count as elements of a person's self-interest, and on whether acting on them is best described as acting against one's self-interest. One could define "self-interest" in a way that makes such a claim false. The important point is that those motives have a distinct explanatory role.

sites. As a consequence, the fishery survived. According to Elinor Ostrom, who has studied this and numerous similar settings, part of the explanation consists in the fact that the anglers tended to respect norms of the kind just mentioned. That is, they assigned weight to fairness, and were disposed to keep agreements, at least under the assumption that others would do so as well. This, together with certain favorable conditions that allowed them to develop a feeling of trust for each other, helped to explain why they managed to reach a consensus on a feasible arrangement, and to comply with it.[32]

The anglers at Alanya solved their problem by changing the structure of their game. The system of allotting fishing sites at Alanya involved fines and sanctions against those who were found not to comply (and measures for monitoring compliance). It might be suggested that this means that the compliance can, after all, be explained in terms of the pursuit to maximize (narrow) self-interest. Let us suppose that this is true. It still does not mean that the dissolution of the dilemma can be explained solely in terms of that aim. For we also must explain the *emergence* of that system, and the fact that it is maintained. And, as many have pointed out, since those actions create public goods, the problem of setting up such a system might in itself constitute a dilemma, a second-order one.[33] For example, according to Ostrom, even if it was better for all of the anglers that the system was established compared to if it had not been, it might still have been better for each not to contribute to the system, whatever the others did.

If Ostrom and the large number of social scientists who reason along similar lines are correct,[34] thus, then certain "social" motives play a crucial role in the explanation of certain important aspects of human behavior. These motives form a class that is assigned a special explanatory role by an adequate account of human behavior, and this, I propose, is the class for which we should reserve the term "moral convictions" within the context of folk psychology and the theory of collective action.[35]

32  See Ostrom's seminal *Governing the Commons*, Chicago: Chicago University Press, 1990, esp. 18–21, 46–49, 183ff, and 211.

33  See, for example, J. Elster, *The Cement of Society: A Study of Social Order*, Cambridge: Cambridge University Press, 1989.

34  See Jane Mansbridge (ed.), *Beyond Self Interest*, Chicago: University of Chicago Press, 1990.

35  I contrast these social motives with the aim to pursue one's self-interest, and assume that they may constitute a constraint on one's willingness to pursue that aim. Again, the plausibility of this picture depends, of course, on what we take an individual's self-interest to consist in. We need not enter into these discussions, however. The important point here is merely

How does this suggestion support the attributional principles to which I have appealed? The idea is that those principles pick out the relevant states. Let us start with the M-constraint. According to the present proposal, the salient feature of moral convictions is that they may permit us to solve social dilemmas. Consider a particular arrangement that helps us to dissolve such a dilemma, and suppose that we consider it to be just. Obviously, the fact that we have this conviction can help to explain why we solve the dilemma only if it motivates us to comply with the arrangement. Similar things can be said about the rest of the moral categories.

What about the Footian constraints? Moral convictions, such as the judgment that a state of affairs is just, help us to dissolve social dilemmas in part since they prompt us to act in some cases in accordance with the interests of others, even if this involves costs in terms of self-interest (narrowly conceived). Such judgments could have this role only if we recognize that the consequences of an arrangement for the well-being of others is relevant to determining whether it *is* just. This explains why we, in accordance with the suggestion by Michael Smith, should translate a sentences of some alien language with our "X is right" only if speakers of the language, in evaluating the sentence assign at least some relevance to the consequences of X to the well-being of others. That is just one example of a Footian constraint. To determine which particular constraints it is reasonable to impose requires more detailed examination of the explanatory role that is assigned to moral judgments within a plausible version of folk psychology.

Finally, consider the latitude idea. In the case of religions, anthropologists have realized that a system of beliefs can have the explanatory role associated with religions even if it does not contain the idea of an omniscient creator. And they have concluded that a system of beliefs need not contain such a belief to count as a religion. Similarly, moral convictions are states that permit us to solve coordination problems, in that they constrain the individual's pursuit of his self-interest. However, many different convictions yield the same result. The fact that the members of some group are utilitarians may permit them to solve some dilemmas (as it prompts them to rank outcomes in the same way). But the same holds for Kantianism, virtue-theory, a right-based morality, as well as a wide range of

that they constitute a class of states that are assigned a special explanatory role in accounting for certain responses to collective action problems.

other rules, conventions and outlooks.[36] In other words, the constraints that make up the class of moral judgments may differ substantially, and different cultures and groups have solved their social dilemmas in different ways. This is why it is reasonable, in identifying the moral judgments of another culture, to allow for considerable latitude. In short, the explanatory role assigned to moral convictions does not exclude that they are different in the sense allowed for by the latitude idea.

Or, in other words, the underlying methodological idea is that, relative to a given theory, some of the differences between items are irrelevant to whether they should be treated as belonging to the same class. For example, the fact that some electrons are located in Sweden, whereas others are located in England, is irrelevant in physical theory. So physical theory has no use for concepts that make those differences explicit – this is a dimension in which differences simply do not matter. The same holds, I propose, for features of our use of moral expressions that undermine the idea that ascriptions of these expressions have the same cognitive contents (in so far as they have any such contents at all). In a way analogous to the differences in location between electrons, differences of that kind are irrelevant to whether the states we express with those expressions can have the explanatory role sketched above – that is to whether they can contribute in the indicated way to the dissolution of social dilemmas. Therefore, the fact that we have a concept of the thought that an action is right or just, and so on, that entails that two thinkers can share that thought even if it cannot plausibly be held to have the same truth condition for both thinkers is not a reason to revise the concept. And this is exactly what the latitude idea is about.

## 6.11. CONCLUSION

What I have argued in this chapter is, in effect, that moral realism conflicts with certain independently justifiable attributional principles. In particular, I have focused on the latitude idea, according to which genuine moral disagreement is not ruled out by differences and circumstances that, given any plausible view on cognitive content, rules out the possibility of

---

36  Many versions of these theories are agent-relative. This means that there are cases in which they may *cause* dilemmas rather than have us avoid them. But this does not rule out that, in other important cases, they may allow agents to find solutions to social dilemmas (e.g., by setting up adequate institutions, etc.). The salient feature is that they in *some* important contexts may contribute to the fact that a group avoids social dilemmas.

genuine disagreement over specific matters of fact. This principle spells trouble for realism as well as for cognitivism more generally.[37]

One reason why it spells trouble for realism is that it denies realists a way of responding to certain traditional antirealist arguments that appeal to moral disagreement. All these arguments presuppose that many moral disagreements are *radical*. The strategy that the latitude idea denies the realist is to explain away such disagreements as *merely apparent*. Because that strategy might be available in other areas, this is part of the explanation of why the latitude idea represents or captures the contrast between ethics and discourses that should be construed in a realist way.

But the more general explanation of why the latitude idea squares badly with realism is that this principle shows, when combined with the other attributional principles to which I have appealed, that in order for a translation manual that represents others as having moral convictions to be correct, it is neither necessary nor sufficient that the sentences with which it translates our ethical sentences express the same beliefs (beliefs with the same truth conditions). Realism, by contrast, implies that this is *both* necessary *and* sufficient. Therefore, it is incompatible with the latitude idea. And because there is, as I have argued, independent support for the latitude idea, we may conclude that realism is false.[38]

Notice, however, that this reasoning is based on a particular understanding of the *content* of moral realism. That is, it is based on the suggestions that were stated in Chapter 1. Thus, realism is not just conceived, say, as the claim that it holds for the ethical sentences of some particular language (such as English) that they express beliefs (for some speakers), and that some of these beliefs are true. Rather, it entails that ethics is a distinct subject matter, which consists of a distinct set of properties or states of affairs, and these are the states of affairs that the ethical sentences of *any* language purport to represent. Metaphorically put, according to this view, if a given sentence is ethical, another sentence may legitimately be translated with it only if it represents the same state of affairs. This is why

37  Remember that it does not help the cognitivist to give up absolutism and adopt some form of relativism. Such a view is not incompatible with the latitude idea. However, by adopting relativism a cognitivist deprives himself of a crucial argument for cognitivism; that is, the argument that cognitivism better than its competitors account for the objectivity of moral judgment. (See further Section 5.9.)

38  Notice that this argument against realism is really quite congenial with Crispin Wright's. For, given the latitude idea, it is the fact that ethics allows for the possibility of radical and widespread disagreement that provides the contrast between realism and areas for which realism is defensible. What is left out in Wright's argument, however, is an explanation of *why* this is so.

realists are committed to thinking that manuals that translate sentences with our ethical sentences must preserve cognitive content, and this is why it is incompatible with the latitude idea.

My conclusions about moral realism can obviously be doubted. However, what I have shown beyond doubt, hopefully, is that questions about when to attribute moral judgments are relevant to the debate between moral realism, cognitivism and their competitors, and that this is especially clear in the context of moral disagreement. According to one view, the fact that there is wide disagreement in the world is a hard and neutral empirical fact. This is why attempts to adjudicate meta-ethical debates by appealing to it might seem a promising strategy. Much of what has been said in this book is intended to undermine this simplified picture. Any report to the effect that there is such disagreement implicitly rests on views about when it is reasonable to attribute moral judgments to other people. And these views square better or worse with the meta-ethical positions around which the contemporary debate revolves, which means that assumptions about the existence or possibility of moral disagreement may be questioned on the ground that they beg the question. Whence my proposal: to focus less on reports about the existence of moral disagreement and turn directly to questions about when, and why, we should accept the views on attribution on which they rely.

Finally, I have argued that we should reject realism. Which of its rivals is preferable? In my view, the answer has to be: some form of expressivism. To justify that answer, however, takes another book.[39]

39  For example, if translation manuals that translate ethical sentences are not supposed to preserve cognitive content, what are they to preserve? This raises well-known questions about how to develop an expressivist account of the content of ethical sentences, questions that in turn are intimately related to the Frege-Geach problem. In my view, the best way to proceed is to explore which constraints it is reasonable to impose on adequate translation manuals, and then try to explicate the content of ethical sentences under the assumption that it is whatever such manuals capture. However, in order to assess this proposal, we obviously need to spell it out in detail. Much work needs to be done.

# References

Abreau, D. "On the Theory of Infinitely Repeated Games with Discounting," *Econometrica* 56 (1988), 383–396.

Anscombe, G. E. M. *Intention*. Oxford: Blackwell, 1957.

Asch, S. E. *Social Psychology*. New York: Prentice Hall, 1952.

Ayer, A. *Language, Truth and Logic*. Harmondsworth: Penguin, 1936.

Bennigson, T. "Irresolvable Disagreement and the Case Against Moral Realism," *Southern Journal of Philosophy* 34 (1996), 411–437.

Bergström, L., and Føllesdal, D. "Interview with Donald Davidson," *Theoria* 60 (1994), 207–225.

Blackburn, S. "Moral Realism," in J. Casey (ed.), *Morality and Moral Reasoning*. London: Methuen, 1971, 101–124.

Blackburn, S. *Spreading the Word*. Oxford: Clarendon Press, 1984.

Blackburn, S. "Just Causes," *Philosophical Studies* 61 (1991), 3–17.

Blackburn, S. *Essays in Quasi-Realism*. New York: Oxford University Press, 1993.

Blackburn, S. "Attitudes and Contents," reprinted in *Essays in Quasi-Realism*, 182–197.

Blackburn, S. "Errors and the Phenomenology of Values," reprinted in *Essays in Quasi-Realism*, 149–165.

Blackburn, S. "The Flight to Reality," in R. Hursthouse, G. Lawrence, and W. Quinn (eds.), *Virtues and Reasons*. Oxford: Clarendon Press, 1995, 35–75.

Blackburn, S. *Ruling Passions*. Oxford: Clarendon Press, 1998.

Block, N. "Functional Role and Truth Conditions," *Proceedings of the Aristotelian Society*, Supp. Vol. 61 (1987), 157–181.

Block, N. "An Advertisement for a Semantics for Psychology," reprinted in S. Stich and T. Warfield (eds), *Mental Representation: A Reader*. Oxford: Blackwell, 1994.

Bloomfield, P. "The Rules of 'Goodness': An Essay on Moral Semantics," *American Philosophical Quarterly* 40 (2003), 197–213.

BonJour, L. *The Structure of Empirical Knowledge*. Cambridge, MA: Harvard University Press, 1985.

Boyd, R. "How to Be a Moral Realist," in G. Sayre-McCord (ed.), *Essays on Moral Realism*. Ithaca, NY: Cornell University Press, 1988, 181–228.

Brandt, R. *Hopi Ethics: A Theoretical Analysis*. Chicago: University of Chicago Press, 1954.

133

Brink, D. O. *Moral Realism and the Foundations of Ethics.* New York: Cambridge University Press, 1989.

Burge, T. "Individualism and the Mental," in P. French, T. Uehling, and H. Wettstein (eds.), *Midwest Studies in Philosophy* 4, Minneapolis: University of Minnesota Press, 1979, 73–121.

Burge, T. "Individualism and Psychology," *Philosophical Review* 95 (1986), 3–45.

Chagnon, N. A., and Hames, R. "Protein Deficiency and Tribal Warfare in Amazonia: New Data," *Science* 203 (1979), 910–913.

Chagnon, N. *Yanomamö: The Fierce People* (5th ed.). Fort Worth: Harcourt, 1997.

Cohen, D., and Nisbett, R. *Culture of Honor: The Psychology of Violence in the South.* Boulder, CO: Westview Press, 1996.

Cohen, D., Nisbett, R., Bowdle, B., Schwarz, N. "Insult, Aggression, and the Southern Culture of Honor: An 'Experimental Ethnography,'" *Journal of Personality and Social Psychology* 70 (1996), 945–960.

Conee, E., and Feldman, R. "The Generality Problem for Reliabilism," *Philosophical Studies* 89 (1998), 1–29.

Cook, J. *Morality and Cultural Differences.* New York: Oxford University Press, 1999.

Cooper, D. "Moral Relativism," *Midwest Studies in Philosophy* 3 (1978), 97–108.

Copp, D. "Milk, Honey, and the Good Life on Moral Twin Earth," *Synthese* 124 (2000), 113–137.

Copp, D. "Realist-Expressivism: A Neglected Option for Moral Realism," *Social Philosophy and Policy* 18 (2001), 1–43.

Dancy, J. *Moral Reasons.* Oxford: Blackwell, 1993.

Daniels, N. "Wide Reflective Equilibrium and Theory Acceptance in Ethics," *Journal of Philosophy* 76 (1979), 256–282.

Darwall, S., Gibbard, A., Railton, P. "Toward *Fin de siècle* Ethics," *Philosophical Review* 101 (1992), 115–189.

Davidson, D. "Toward a Unified Theory of Meaning and Action," *Grazer Philosophische Studien* 11 (1980), 1–12.

Davidson, D. *Inquiries into Truth and Interpretation.* Oxford: Clarendon Press, 1984.

Davidson, D. *Expressing Evaluations*, The Lindley Lecture, published as monograph. Lawrence: University of Kansas, 1984.

Davidson, D. "A New Basis for Decision Theory," *Theory and Decision* 18 (1985), 87–98.

Davidson, D. "The Structure and Content of Truth," *Journal of Philosophy* 87 (1990), 279–328.

Davidson, D. "On Quine's Philosophy'," *Theoria* 60 (1994), 184–192.

Davidson, D. "The Objectivity of Values," in C. Gutierrez (ed.), *El Trabajo Filosofico de Hoy en el Continente.* Bogota: Editorial ABC, 1995, 59–69.

Davidson, D. "Objectivity and Practical Reason," in E. Ullman-Margalit (ed.), *Reasoning Practically.* Oxford: Oxford University Press, 2000, 17–26.

Davidson, D. *Subjective, Intersubjective, Objective*, Oxford: Oxford University Press, 2001.

Davidson, D. "The Myth of the Subjective," reprinted in *Subjective, Intersubjective, Objective*, 39–53.

Davson-Galle, P. "Arguing, Arguments, and Deep Disagreements," *Journal of Informal Logic* 14 (1992), 147–156.

Doris, J. M., and Stich, S. P. "As a Matter of Fact: Empirical Perspectives on Ethics," in F. Jackson, and M. Smith (eds.), *The Oxford Handbook of Contemporary Analytic Philosophy*, Oxford: Oxford University Press, forthcoming.

Dworkin, R. "Objectivity and Truth. You'd Better Believe It," *Philosophy & Public Affairs* 25 (1996), 87–139.

Dworkin, R. "Reply to Critics." BEARS, J. Dreier and D. Estlund (eds.), http://www.brown.edu/Departments/Philosophy/bears/homepage.html. Posted September 4, 1997.

Dummett, M. *Truth and Other Enigmas*. London: Duckworth, 1978.

Edney, J. "Freeriders en Route to Disaster," *Psychology Today* 13 (1979), 80–112.

Elster, J. *The Cement of Society: A Study of Social Order*. Cambridge: Cambridge University Press, 1989.

Falk, W. D., "'Ought' and Motivation," *Proceedings of the Aristotelian Society* 48 (1947–1948), 492–510.

Feldman, R. "Logic, Meaning and Conceptual Role," *Journal of Philosophy* 69 (1977), 379–408.

Feldman, R. "Reliability and Justification," *Monist* 68 (1985), 159–174.

Field, H. "Logic, Meaning and Conceptual Role," *Journal of Philosophy* 69 (1977), 379–408.

Field, H. "The Deflationary Conception of Truth," in G. MacDonald, and C. Wright (eds.), *Fact, Science and Morality*, Oxford: Blackwell, 1986, 55–117.

Foot, P. *Virtues and Vices*. Oxford: Blackwell, 1978.

Frankena, W. "Obligation and Motivation in Recent Moral Philosophy," in A. Melden (ed.), *Essays in Moral Philosophy*. Seattle: University of Washington Press, 1958, 40–81.

Føllesdal, D. "The Status of Rationality Assumptions in Interpretation and in the Explanation of Action," *Dialectica* 36 (1982), 301–316.

Gallie, W. B. "Essentially Contested Concepts," *Proceedings of the Aristotelian Society* 56 (1955–1956), 167–198.

Gallie, W. B. *Philosophy and Historical Understanding*. London: Chatto and Windus, 1964.

Geach, P. T. "Assertion," *Philosophical Review* 74 (1965), 449–465.

Gibbard, A. *Wise Choices, Apt Feelings*. Oxford: Clarendon Press, 1990.

Gibbard, A. *Thinking How to Live*. Cambridge, MA: Harvard University Press, 2003.

Goldman, A. H. *Moral Knowledge*. London: Routledge, 1988.

Goldman, A. I "What Is Justified Belief?," in G. Pappas (ed.), *Justification and Knowledge*. Dordrecht: Reidel, 1979, 1–23.

Gowans, C. W. (ed.), *Moral Disagreements: Classic and Contemporary Readings*. London: Routledge, 1999.

Grandy, R. "Reference, Belief and Meaning," *Journal of Philosophy* 70 (1973), 439–452.

Greene, J. D., Sommerville, R. B., Nystrom, L. E., Darley, J. M. and Cohen, J. D. "An fMRI Investigation of Emotional Engagement in Moral Judgment," *Science* 293 (2001), 2105–2108.

Hardin, G. "The Tragedy of the Commons," *Science* 162 (1968), 1243–1248.

Hare, R. *The Language of Morals*. Oxford: Clarendon Press, 1952.

Hare, R. "A 'Reductio Ad Absurdum' of Descriptivism," in S. Shanker (ed.), *Philosophy in Britain Today*, London: Croom Helm, 1986, 118–136.

Harman, G. "Moral Relativism Defended," *Philosophical Review* 84 (1975), 3–22.

Harman, G. *The Nature of Morality*. New York: Oxford University Press, 1977.

Harman, G. "Moral Explanations of Natural Facts – Can Moral Claims Be Tested Against Moral Reality?," *Southern Journal of Philosophy* 24 (suppl.) (1986), 57–68.

Harman, G. "Moral Philosophy and Linguistics," in K. Brinkmann (ed.), *Proceedings of the 20th World Congress of Philosophy, Volume I: Ethics*. Bowling Green, Ohio: Philosophy Documentation Center, 1999, 107–115.

Harms, W. F. "Adaptation and Moral Realism," *Biology and Philosophy* 15 (2000), 699–712.

Harris, M. *Cannibals and Kings*. New York: Random House, 1977.

Harris, M. "Animal Capture and Yanamamo Warfare: Retrospect and New Evidence," *Journal of Anthropological Research* 40 (1984), 183–201.

Herskovits, M. *Cultural Anthropology*. New York: Knopf, 1955.

Horgan, T., and Timmons, M. "New Wave Moral Realism Meets Moral Twin Earth," *Journal of Philosophical Research* 16 (1990–1991), 447–465.

Horgan, T., and Timmons, M. "Troubles on Moral Twin Earth," *Synthese* 92 (1992), 221–260.

Horgan, T., and Timmons, M. "From Moral Realism to Moral Relativism in One Easy Step," *Critica* 28 (1996), 3–39.

Horgan, T., and Timmons, M. "Copping Out on Moral Twin Earth," *Synthese* 124 (2000), 139–152.

Hurley, S. "Objectivity and Disagreement," in T. Honderich (ed.), *Morality and Objectivity*. London: Routledge & Kegan Paul, 1985, 54–97.

Hurley. S. *Natural Reasons*, Oxford: Oxford University Press, 1989.

Jackson, F. *From Metaphysics to Ethics*. Oxford: Clarendon Press, 1998.

Jackson, F., and Pettit, P. "A Problem for Expressivism," *Analysis* 58 (1998), 239–251.

Joyce, R. *The Myth of Morality*. New York: Cambridge University Press, 2001.

Joyce, R. "Moral Realism and Teleosemantics," *Biology and Philosophy* 16 (2001), 725–734.

Kripke, S. *Naming and Necessity*. Oxford: Blackwell, 1980.

Lehrer, K. *Theory of Knowledge*. London: Routledge, 1990.

Lenman, J. "The Externalist and the Amoralist," *Philosophia* 27 (1999), 441–457.

Lewis, D. "Radical Interpretation," *Philosophical Papers* (Vol. 1). Oxford: Oxford University Press, 1983, 108–121.

Lind, J. T. "Do the Rich Vote Conservative because They Are Rich?" http://folk.uio.no/jlind/papers/PartyInc.pdf.

Loeb, D. "Moral Realism and the Argument from Disagreement," *Philosophical Studies* 90 (1998), 281–303.

Lukes, S. "Relativism in its Place," in M. Hollis and S. Lukes (eds.), *Rationality and Relativism*. Oxford: Blackwell, 1982, 261–305.

Mackie, J. *Ethics. Inventing Right and Wrong*. New York: Penguin, 1977.

Mansbridge, J. (ed.), *Beyond Self-Interest*. Chicago: University of Chicago Press, 1990.

McDowell, J. "Are Moral Requirements Hypothetical Imperatives?," *Proceedings of the Aristotelian Society* 52 (Suppl.) (1978) 13–29.

McDowell, J. "Values and Secondary Qualities," in T. Honderich (ed.), *Morality and Objectivity*. London: Routledge, & Kegan Paul, 1985, 110–129.

Merli, D. "Return to Moral Twin Earth," *Canadian Journal of Philosophy* 32 (2002), 207–240.

Miller, R. *Moral Differences*. Princeton, NJ: Princeton University Press, 1992.

Millikan, R. *Language, Thought and Other Biological Categories*. Cambridge, MA: MIT Press, 1984.

Milo, R. D. "Moral Deadlock," *Philosophy* 61 (1986), 453–471.

Moore, G. E. *Ethics*. London: Oxford University Press, 1912.

Newton-Smith, W. *The Rationality of Science*. London: Routledge, 1981.

Ostrom, E. *Governing the Commons*. Chicago: Chicago University Press, 1990.

Ostrom, E. "A Behavioral Approach to the Rational Choice Theory of Collective Action," *American Political Science Review* 92 (1998), 1–22.

Parfit, D. *Reasons and Persons*. Oxford: Oxford University Press, 1984.

Pettit, P. "Embracing Objectivity in Ethics," in Leiter, B. (ed.), *Objectivity in Law and Morals*. Cambridge: Cambridge University Press, 2001, 234–286.

Pollock, J. L. "Reliability and Justified Belief," *Canadian Journal of Philosophy* 14 (1984), 103–114.

Putnam, H. "The Meaning of 'Meaning'," in *Mind, Language, and Reality*. Cambridge: Cambridge University Press, 1975, 215–271.

Quine, W. V. O. *Word and Object*. Cambridge, MA: MIT Press, 1960.

Quine, W. V. O. "Two Dogmas of Empiricism," reprinted in *From a Logical Point of View* (2nd ed.). New York: Harper & Row, 1961, 20–46.

Quine, W. V. O. "Epistemology Naturalized," in *Ontological Relativity*. New York: Columbia University Press, 1969, 69–90.

Quine, W. V. O. "On the Nature of Moral Values," reprinted in *Theories and Things*. Cambridge, MA: Harvard University Press, 1981, 55–66.

Ross, W. D. *The Right and the Good*. Oxford: Oxford University Press, 1930.

Ryan, J. "Moral Relativism and the Argument from Moral Disagreement," *Journal of Social Philosophy* 34 (2003), 377–386.

Salwén, H. *Hume's Law*. Stockholm: Almqvist & Wiksell, 2003.

Sayre-McCord, G. "The Many Moral Realisms," in G. Sayre-McCord, (ed.), *Essays on Moral Realism*. Ithaca, NY: Cornell University Press, 1988, 1–23.

Sayre-McCord, G. "Being a Realist about Relativism (in Ethics)," *Philosophical Studies* 61 (1991), 155–176.

Scanlon, T. *What We Owe to Each Other*. Cambridge, MA: Belknap Press, 1999.

Scheuler, G. F. "Modus Ponens and Moral Realism," *Ethics* 98 (1988), 492–500.

Sextus Empiricus, *Outlines of Scepticism* (Julia Annas's and Jonathan Barnes's edition). Cambridge: Cambridge University Press, 1994.

Shafer-Landau, R. "Ethical Disagreement, Ethical Objectivism and Moral Indeterminacy," *Philosophy and Phenomenological Research* 54 (1994), 331–344.

Shafer-Landau, R. "Vagueness, Borderline Cases and Moral Realism," *American Philosophical Quarterly* 32 (1995), 83–96.

Sherif, M. *The Psychology of Social Norms*. New York: Harper & Row, 1936.

Singer, P. "How Reliable are our Moral Intuitions?," *Free Inquiry* 23 (2003), 19–20.

Smart, J. J. C. *Ethics, Persuasion and Truth*. London: Routledge & Kegan Paul, 1984.

Smith, M. "Objectivity and Moral Realism. On the Significance of the Phenomenology of Moral Experience," in J. Haldane and C. Wright (eds.), *Reality, Representation and Projection*. Oxford: Oxford University Press, 1993, 235–255.

Smith, M. *The Moral Problem*. Oxford: Blackwell, 1994.

Sosa, E. "The Raft and the Pyramid: Coherence versus Foundations in the Theory of Knowledge," in P. French, T. Uehling & H. Wettstein (eds.), *Midwest Studies in Philosophy* 5, Notre Dame: University of Notre Dame Press, 1980, 3–25.

Stevenson, C. L. *Ethics and Language*. New Haven, CT: Yale University Press, 1944.

Stevenson, C. L. *Facts and Values*. New Haven, CT: Yale University Press, 1963.

Stout, J. *Ethics After Babel*. Boston: Beacon Press, 1988.

Sturgeon, N. "What Difference Does It Make Whether Moral Realism is True?," *Southern Journal of Philosophy* 24 (Suppl.) (1986), 115–141.

Sturgeon, N. "Moral Explanations," reprinted in G. Sayre-McCord (ed.), *Essays on Moral Realism*. Ithaca, NY: Cornell University Press, 1988, 229–255.

Sturgeon, N. "Contents and Causes," *Philosophical Studies* 61 (1991), 19–37.

Sturgeon, N. "Moral Disagreement and Moral Relativism," *Social Philosophy and Policy* 11 (1994), 80–115.

Tersman, F. "Utilitarianism and the Idea of Reflective Equilibrium," *Southern Journal of Philosophy* 29 (1991), 395–406.

Tersman, F. "Coherence and Disagreement," *Philosophical Studies* 65 (1992), 305–317.

Tersman, F. *Reflective Equilibrium. An Essay in Moral Epistemology*. Stockholm: Almqvist & Wiksell, 1993.

Tersman, F. "Crispin Wright on Moral Disagreement," *Philosophical Quarterly* 48 (1998), 359–365.

Tersman, F. "Quine on Ethics," *Theoria* 64 (1998), 84–98.

Tersman, F. "Are We Lovers of the Good?," *Synthese* 138 (2004), 247–260.

Tierney, P. *Darkness in El Dorado: How Scientists and Journalists Devastated the Amazon*. London and New York: W.W. Norton & Company, 2000.

Tolhurst, W. "The Argument from Moral Disagreement," *Ethics* 97 (1987), 610–621.

Turnbull, C. *The Mountain People*. New York: Simon & Schuster, 1972.

Wedgwood, R. "Conceptual Role Semantics for Moral Terms," *Philosophical Review* 110 (2001), 1–30.

Westermarck, E. *Ethical Relativity*. New York: Harcourt, Brace and Company, 1932.

Wiggins, D. "Truth, Invention and the Meaning of Life," in *Needs, Values, Truth: Essays in the Philosophy of Value*. Oxford: Blackwell, 1987, 87–138.

Williams, B. *Ethics and the Limits of Philosophy*. London: Fontana, 1985.

Williamson, T. *Vagueness*. London: Routledge, 1994.

Williamson, T. "A Critical Study of *Truth and Objectivity*," *International Journal of Philosophical Studies* 1 (1993), 130–144.

Wong, D. *Moral Relativity*. Berkeley: University of California Press, 1984.

Wright, C. *Truth and Objectivity*. Cambridge, MA: Harvard University Press, 1992.

Wright, C. "Realism: Pure and Simple?," *International Journal of Philosophical Studies* 2 (1994), 327–341.

Wright, C. "Truth in Ethics," in B. Hooker (ed.), *Truth in Ethics*. Oxford: Blackwell, 1996, 1–18.

Wright, C. "On Being in Quandary," *Mind* 110 (2001), 45–98.

# Index

Lightning Source UK Ltd.
Milton Keynes UK
UKOW03f0229030517

300381UK00001B/63/P